To Jim

HOW PROTESTANTS DIFFER
FROM ROMAN CATHOLICS

from m/m Gene Thompson

AN ADAPTATION

from the author's full length

Primer on Roman Catholicism for Protestants

How Protestants Differ
from Roman Catholics

STANLEY I. STUBER

ASSOCIATION PRESS · NEW YORK

HOW PROTESTANTS DIFFER
FROM ROMAN CATHOLICS

Price, 50 cents

Library of Congress catalog card number: 61-7112

Printed in the United States of America

This book is DEDICATED to those who give ecumenical leadership at the grass-root level of American life—the executives of city and metropolitan councils of churches.

ACKNOWLEDGMENTS

Appreciation is expressed for permission to quote from the following publications having the official *Nihil obstat* and *Imprimatur* of the Roman Catholic Church: The Confraternity of Christian Doctrine, Washington, D.C., for permission to quote from Father McGuire's *New Baltimore Catechism and Mass*, No. 2, Official Revised Edition, and the Revised Edition of the *Baltimore Catechism*, No. 2; Saint Anthony's Guild Press, Paterson, New Jersey, for permission to quote from the *1952 National Catholic Almanac*, and *The Cathechism of Christian Doctrine*, No. 3, Revised Edition; the Paulist Press, New York City, for permission to quote from papal encyclical letters, from *Are Anglican Ministers Catholic Priests?* by F. Woodlock, *The Popes, Infallible Teachers* by J. B. Harney, and *The Question Box* by B. L. Conway; and the Our Sunday Visitor Press, Huntington, Indiana, for permission to quote from *The Faith of Millions* by John A. O'Brien.

Also to M. H. Gill & Son, Ltd., Dublin, Ireland, for permission to quote from *Apologetics and Catholic Doctrine*, Second and Revised Edition; The Macmillan Company, New York City, for permission to quote from *A Catholic Dictionary*, edited by Donald Attwater, copyrighted 1949; and P. J. Kenedy & Sons, New York City, for permission to quote from Cardinal Gibbons' *Faith of Our Fathers*.

Appreciation is also expressed to G. P. Putnam's Sons for permission to quote from *Our Fathers' Faith and Ours* by David Schaff.

S.I.S.

PREFACE

The former Archbishop of Canterbury, Dr. William Temple, called the ecumenical movement the great new fact of our modern era. If he could have lived to witness the present currents of cooperation between the Eastern Orthodox Church and Protestant churches within the World Council of Churches, the visit of his successor to the pope at the Vatican, the union of denominations and the proposal for a new church "both Catholic and Reformed," the election of a Roman Catholic as president of the United States of America, the emphasis upon church union at the "Ecumenical Council" called by Pope John XXIII, and a wave of "dialogues" between Protestants and Roman Catholics in Europe and here, Archbishop Temple would have indeed rejoiced. We are now in a fluid, exciting period of church history, when the unexpected may well happen.

This book therefore deals with the outstanding differences between Protestants and Roman Catholics, from a constructive, creative point of view. It is frankly admitted that there are basic differences, and the differences are stated as simply and as clearly as possible. It is the author's contention that only as we look realistically and factually at the actual differences will we ever be able to make progress toward any kind of true Christian co-operation, understanding, and unity.

Therefore this book is based upon these propositions:

1. That both Protestants and Roman Catholics work together toward the fulfillment of basic Christian principles as found in the New Testament.

2. That both sides encourage the current "dialogue" in order to arrive, if possible, at a better understanding of each other's real position.

3. That Protestants and Roman Catholics recognize each other as fully committed to Christianity and proceed to formulate the best possible ecclesiastical, theological, and practical relationships.

In view of the variety of opinions held by Protestants, and the various interpretations of Roman Catholic doctrines, this book cannot possibly give full, complete answers to all the questions raised. We have attempted a more adequate discussion in our *Primer on Roman Catholicism for Protestants*. It should also be noted that increasingly, on both sides, there is developing a broader interpretation of certain doctrines, which increases the difficulty in claiming any single interpretation as absolutely representative of a particular group. However, it is felt that the statements here accurately represent the prevailing thought and practice of each group.

Supporting this book is the hope that all Christians—Protestants, Orthodox, and Roman Catholics—may in the next decade or two make much progress in the direction of understanding and unity. Whether this will lead ultimately to one great church is, of course, quite another matter. Pope John XXIII has attempted to prepare the way, in his "Ecumenical Council," for a return to the "one true church." Few non-Catholics will submit to the ground rules laid down by the Pope. There are certain indications, however, that Protestants and Roman Catholics are now ready to examine each other critically—for the purpose not of destroying, but of saving, each other. New forms of Christian relationship, within the Church Universal, are in the making.

Stanley I. Stuber

Kansas City, Mo.

1. *Protestants believe that membership in the Church extends to all true Christians and that the Church is "a community of forgiven sinners";[1] Roman Catholics believe that the Church's membership is restricted to those who are members of the Roman Catholic Church, either knowingly or unknowingly.*

According to Roman Catholics, Christ himself founded the Church in the form of a visible, hierarchical society, being made up of subjects and superiors. The Roman Catholic Church teaches that a person becomes a member of the Church upon receiving the sacrament of Baptism. To remain a real member, he then must continue to profess the one true faith and must not withdraw from the unity of the body of the Church by schism or heresy, or be excommunicated because

---

[1] All quotations relating to Protestantism, other than those identified, are taken from *Faith and Order,* the official report of the Third World Conference at Lund, 1952.

of serious sins. The teaching that "outside the Church there is no salvation" does not mean that everyone who is not a Roman Catholic will necessarily go to hell, but it does mean that no person can be saved unless he belongs in some manner to the Roman Catholic Church—either actually or *in desire*, which may be unconscious.

"No one can be saved without sanctifying grace, and the Catholic Church alone is the divinely established means by which grace is brought to the world and the full fruits of Our Lord's Redemption are applied to men" (*A Catechism of Christian Doctrine*,[2] p. 129).

The Roman Catholic Church is declared to be the Mystical Body of Christ because "its members are united by supernatural bonds with one another and with Christ, their Head, thus resembling the members and head of the living human body" (*A Catechism of Christian Doctrine*, p. 129).

According to a résumé of beliefs formulated and

---

[2] *A Catechism of Christian Doctrine*, No. 3, Official Revised Edition, represents Catechism No. 2, Revised Edition of the *Baltimore Catechism*, with supplementary statements and quotations from Holy Scripture. This text is used throughout the book by permission of the Confraternity of Christian Doctrine.

adopted by the Protestant delegates at Lund, Protestants also think of the Church as being founded by Christ at Pentecost, but they conceive it to be more a spiritual fellowship. They do not discover in the New Testament any statement which would indicate that the Church must be organized as one visible body under the sole rule of a pope. They do, however, find much evidence supporting the belief that the true Church is of the Spirit; is of *all* those who love Christ and obey his commandments. This was stressed in 1960, both by the Central Committee of the World Council of Churches and in the "Message to the Member Churches" of the Fifth General Assembly of the National Council of the Churches of Christ in the U.S.A.

The Roman Catholic Church regards the Kingdom as equivalent to and coextensive with the Church, whereas in Protestantism the Kingdom and the Church are not necessarily one and the same thing. The Kingdom of God, which Jesus emphasized so much, is the concern of Protestants; and membership in the visible Church here on earth is not ipso facto membership in the Kingdom. All earnest Christians—Eastern Orthodox, Roman Catholics, and Protestants alike—who are born into the Kingdom are equally redeemed and equally beyond the visible churches which, for the moment, separate us.

ॐ

2. *Protestants believe that only "Christ is head of the Church which is His Body"; Roman Catholics believe that the pope is ruler of the visible Church on earth as the Vicar of Christ.*

The Roman Catholic Church has taught, since the eleventh century, that Christ made Peter the first head of the Church, the first Roman Pontiff. The Church is a monarchical society in which the pope rules with full power, having jurisdiction over the entire Church.

Christ gave special power to Peter, Roman Catholics believe, by making him the head of the apostles and the chief teacher and ruler over the entire Church. The power of the keys (Matt. 16:17-19) was promised to Peter and was actually conferred upon him (John 21:15-17). He was recognized by the early Christians from the very beginning, as the head of the Church (*A Catechism of Christian Doctrine,* p. 111).

The Roman Catholic Church believes that Christ did not intend that the special power of chief teacher and ruler of the entire Church should be exercised by Peter alone. This power was to be passed on from one bishop of Rome to another pope, who would serve on earth as the Vicar of Christ. The popes, along with the other bishops, are the successors of the apostles and have received their episcopal power by valid consecration through an unbroken line of successors of the apostles. Priests, especially parish priests, assist the bishop in the care of souls (*A Catechism of Christian Doctrine*, pp. 112-113).

Protestants differ widely in regard to rites and practices, but they are united in the belief that salvation comes not exclusively through the rites of the Church, but through the grace of God manifested in Jesus Christ. As long as the Roman Catholic Church insists that salvation must be found in the "one true Church," so long will the principles of the Protestant Reformation be proclaimed in protest. Protestants are *testifying* for great spiritual principles as their name (*pro testare*) indicates they should. Protestant beliefs are based upon deep, personal religious experience inspired by the Christian heritage and lead to God directly through Jesus

Christ. Protestant churches carry their origins back directly to the New Testament and claim Christ as their Founder and Head.

ॐ

3. *Protestants emphasize justification by faith— that salvation comes directly of God; Roman Catholics believe that salvation is secured by faith plus good works—as channeled through the Roman Catholic Church.*[3]

The Council of Trent was called to settle the controversies growing out of the Protestant "revolt." It met in December, 1545, and lasted for eighteen years. During that time the Council did more than define the doctrines which had been brought into question by Protestants. It also gave explicit directions for reform where reform was needed, and supplied an example of the inner vitality and unity of the Church.

Members of the Council discussed the dogmatic

---

[3] The extreme views which originally characterized this issue—when such "works" as indulgences were being held up as a means of salvation—now, for the most part, no longer prevail on either side.

questions with great frankness and thoroughness. They devoted, for example, six full months to the study of justification, the central doctrine of Protestantism. After reaching a decision they rejected the "errors" of their opponents in no uncertain terms. According to the *Catholic Dictionary*, edited by Donald Attwater, one of the principal decisions reached at the Council of Trent is as follows: "The precision of the doctrine of Justification, condemning justification by faith alone and imputation of grace."

The Roman Catholic Church believes in good works, along with faith, and as an expression of faith. Moreover, it believes that good works can help the Christian gain eternal rewards. It plainly teaches that "without faith it is impossible to be saved" (*A Catechism of Christian Doctrine,* p. 91). Yet it says that good works must be added to faith, to prove that the faith is alive.

One of the declarations propounded for the faithful in *A Catechism of Christian Doctrine* reads: "Our Lord taught explicitly that one can earn the eternal reward of heaven by performing the corporal works of mercy and that those who deliberately refuse to perform such good works will be barred from heaven" (p. 152).

Roman Catholics have the poor very much at heart. In their churches they have alms boxes prominently displayed. Charity with them is not only a part of good works in which there is merit, but also a demonstration that the Roman Catholic Church itself is on the side of the poor. Pope Pius XI, in his encyclical letter *Divini Redemptoris*, calls for the practice of charity and help for the poor. "Sinful pleasures must be renounced and self must be forgotten for love of thy neighbor," the pope says. "There is a divine regenerating force in the New Commandment, as Christ calls charity. Its faithful observance will bring peace to the heart of the individual and to the world."

Everyone in the Roman Catholic Church is obliged to perform works of mercy. They vary according to the ability of the members and needs of the neighbors. All of the ordinary deeds which are done day by day to relieve the need of others are works of mercy, if they are done in the name of Christ.

The Roman Catholic Church teaches that there is merit in good works, reward resting not in the works themselves but on the promise of Christ that he will reward faithful servants of his. If good deeds are done in his honor and service, aided always by divine grace, they are meritorious. St. Augustine is quoted as saying, "When God crowns our merits, He crowns His own gifts."

Holding that the grace of God is a free gift and cannot be won or bought with a price, Protestantism does not accept the Roman Catholic doctrine of "good works." Protestants also believe that works must be added to faith, and some have even declared that works precedent to justification are legitimate if not necessary.

Good works, while not being a factor in obtaining eternal salvation, have always had a leading part in Protestant practice, since the application of the Gospel message is found to be a fundamental teaching of Scripture. Luther, for example, in his *Freedom of a Christian Man* declares: "Good works do not make a man good, but a good man doeth good works. True faith is a lively thing and can in no wise be idle. Therefore, teach we the people that God hath called us not to follow riot and wantonness but, as Paul said, 'He hath called us unto good works to walk in them.' "

Protestants have never rejected Christian charity. What they have opposed is the attempt to make salvation rest upon the winning of merits and not upon the free will of a just and loving God. Once one has been redeemed by the grace of God, and justified by faith, then there should be a constant flow of deeds of kindness and manifestation of love.

ॐ

4. *Protestants believe that the Protestant Reformation was a return to the creative faith of the New Testament; Roman Catholics think of the Reformation as something forced upon a self-reforming Church and as alien to the true Christian faith.*

To Roman Catholics, Martin Luther is a heretic, a rebel against the true Church. The denominations which grew out of his rebellion are not true churches at all and will have no divine authority until they are reunited with Rome.

From the Council of Trent proceeded a force "of order, of holiness, of firmness, of purpose, of unity, of Catholicity. It was ultimately to cleanse and remake Catholic society, and regain many of the souls lost in the Protestant revolt" (*Church History Through Biography*, published by the Confraternity of Christian doctrine, p. 144).

Many feel that there is great need today for Protestants to re-examine those theological statements and creeds that tend to divide. For others, the hope of the Protestant churches is not in the process of redefining dogmas which separate, but in building around the creative elements of the Reformation which will send all earnest Christians forth to fulfill the basic principles of the Kingdom of God.

From the very beginning Protestantism was never a protest against the Church itself; it was a protest against certain abuses within the Christian body. It should be emphasized that Protestants have never separated themselves from the Holy Catholic Church. This is evident every time the Apostles' Creed is repeated in Protestant churches. Protestants do not intend to forfeit the word "catholic" when it means universal, world-wide, or a global fellowship. Protestantism's catholicity is found in one Christ, in one Bible, in one Holy Spirit, in one Kingdom.

The Protestant Reformation had its birth and inspiration in Holy Scripture. The central verse of the Reformation was: "The just shall live by faith" (Rom. 1:17b). This is the scriptural basis for the great Reformation principle, "justification by faith." Moreover, the Bible itself tended to become the sole necessity for faith, life, and salvation for Protestantism. This is why Chillingworth declared: "The Bible and the Bible alone is the religion of Protestants."

Scripture passages which formed a solid foundation for the Protestant Reformation are: "For by grace are ye saved through faith; and that not of yourselves; it is the gift of God; not of works" (Eph. 2:8, 9). "Stand fast therefore in the liberty wherewith Christ hath made us free, and be not entangled again with the yoke of bondage (Gal. 5:1).

ᏸᏴ

5. *Protestants believe that no human being is, or can be, infallible; the Roman Catholic Church teaches that when the pope speaks* ex cathedra *he is infallible.*

The pope is misunderstood by many Protestants. They fail to see his limitations. They think of him as having absolute authority over approximately 500,000,000 Catholics around the world. They do not realize that the pope, from the Roman Catholic point of view, is merely a man, a man who can sin, who can make mistakes and is therefore quite fallible, and a man who owes his authority not to his own personal qualifications, but to the position of the office which he holds.

Pronouncements of the Roman Catholic Church have different types of binding authority. When the pope speaks *ex cathedra* in defining a dogma of the church, then this is binding on all Roman Catholics. Other ecclesiastical pronouncements, such as encyclicals, carry great moral weight, but they are not necessarily of an *ex cathedra* nature. Directions issued by the hierarchy are binding in the area of faith and morals, but they are not considered free from possible error or fault.

The Catholic position is stated in *The Popes, Infallible Teachers*, by John B. Harney, C.S.P., published by the Paulist Press (pp. 7-8):

"Our belief is that the Pope, without a single exception, from Peter to Pius XII, has been blessed and protected by Almighty God with the gift of infallibility in the exercise of his Supreme Teaching Authority. To know when this authority is involved, we must pay close attention to the following conditions:

"1. It must be perfectly clear and certain that the Pope is defining, i.e., is handing down a final, authoritative, and irrevocable decision.

23

"2. Concerning a matter of either faith or morals;

"3. And that he means to make his decision binding on all Christians."

Catholics believe that in spite of papal infallibility popes are mortal, sinful men, and have to earn their way to eternal salvation like any other Catholic.

Protestants maintain that the pope has no power and no authority not already granted to other Christian leaders, and that Christians owe no special allegiance to the pope in Rome. Since the entire Roman hierarchy is built upon the opposite position, it is impossible, at this time, for Protestants and Roman Catholics to come to any agreement in regard to the chief authority of the visible Church.

Protestants honor the pope as a great religious leader, and not because he claims to be the Vicar of Christ here upon earth. Their guidance comes directly from Christ. Anything less than this, from the Protestant viewpoint, is a denial of the fundamental principles of the New Testament. Protestants find their authority in the Scriptures, for they believe the Bible to be the Word of God. It speaks to them with divine authority. They believe it and accept it as the most precious and binding authority because they are convinced that, through the Book, God speaks directly to the human soul.

ॐ

6. *Protestants believe that Peter was one of Christ's chief apostles; Roman Catholics believe that he is "the Rock" upon which the Church is founded. Roman Catholics believe in the appointment by Christ of Peter as the first among the apostles. Moreover, they believe that Christ gave to Peter alone special powers. Peter, to them, was the first pope.*

This is the Scripture basis for the Roman Catholic claim that Peter was the first pope: "Then Jesus answered and said, 'Blessed art thou, Simon Barjona, for flesh and blood has not revealed this to thee, but my Father in heaven. And I say to thee, thou art Peter, and upon this rock I will build my Church, and the gates of hell shall not prevail against it. And I will give thee the keys of the kingdom of heaven; and whatever thou shalt bind on earth shall be bound in heaven, and whatever thou shalt loose on earth shall be loosed in heaven' "

(Matt. 16:17-19, from the Revised Challoner-Rheims Version).

Protestants think of Peter as one of the apostles, but with no special authority or powers. They are insistent that Christ is head of the Church, and that there need be no other. They establish their authority not upon a human being but upon the living Word of God. Jesus' words to Peter recorded in Matthew 16:18 and in John 21:15 ("Thou art Peter and upon this rock I will build my church, and the gates of hell shall not prevail against it." . . . "Feed my sheep, feed my lambs.") are not associated with any kind of church organization, but are given an ever new relationship to Christ, the spiritual head of the Church. According to David Schaff, in *Our Fathers' Faith and Ours* (pp. 245-246), the Protestant position in regard to these verses is stated in part as follows: "In the parallel passages of Mark 8:29 and Luke 9:20 Peter is not even mentioned as 'the rock.' " . . . "Christ, and not Peter, in every other place in the New Testament is called the rock, the foundation, the cornerstone of the church. (See I Cor.: 3:11, for example.)" . . . "Peter is never accorded special authority as far as the New Testament is concerned. He is always co-equal in authority with the other apostles. (See Matt. 28:19; I Cor. 12:28; Acts 8:14; Rev. 21:14.)" . . . "James, rather than Peter, presided at the only church council which occurred in apostolic times. (See Acts 15:13.)" Furthermore, Rome herself claimed no unique authority of Peter or infallibility of the pope during the early centuries of Christianity.

ॐ

7. *Protestants believe that, along with the ethics of the Gospels and the Epistles, the Ten Commandments are the basis for individual and social moral behavior; Roman Catholics add to the Ten Commandments the six Precepts of the Church.*

In the Roman Catholic Church the firm basis of moral behavior and the day-by-day practice of basic Christian principles are grounded in a realistic acceptance of the Ten Commandments and what are known as the six Precepts of the Church. Because of space limitations the well-known Ten Commandments (Exod. 20:3-17) are not quoted here. The six Precepts of the Church, which supplement the Ten Commandments by giving additional detailed guidance for personal conduct, follow:

1. To hear Mass on Sundays and holy days of obligation.
2. To fast and abstain on the days appointed.
3. To confess at least once a year.
4. To receive the Holy Eucharist during the Easter time.
5. To contribute to the support of the Church.
6. Not to marry persons who are not Catholics, or who are related to us within the third degree of kindred, nor privately without witnesses, nor to solemnize marriage at forbidden times.

The Ten Commandments are God's laws and must be obeyed as duties directly to God. The Precepts are the commandments of the Church and are equally binding, although not on the same level. Roman Catholics believe that the Church, being the divine representative of Christ, has the right to make laws, and naturally gives her laws the highest possible sanction of binding in conscience under sin.

Protestantism believes that members of the church should be motivated by a Christian conscience, and not by ecclesiastical requirements, to be faithful to their Church. They go directly to the Bible for their moral and social principles. Beginning with the Ten Commandments and the teachings of the prophets, they proceed to the principles of The Sermon on the Mount and to Christ's new commandments: "Thou shalt love the Lord thy God with thy whole heart, and with thy whole soul, and with thy whole mind. This is the greatest and the first commandment. And the second is like it, Thou shalt love thy neighbor as thyself. On these two commandments depend the whole Law and the Prophets" (Matt. 22:35-40).

Protestants join Roman Catholics in the promotion of the moral values inherent in the Ten Commandments and desire to work with them in carrying them to fulfillment in modern life.

8. *Protestants believe in voluntary and conscientious church attendance; Roman Catholics officially require Church attendance as a spiritual necessity.*

Church attendance, from the Protestant point of view, is motivated by a series of desires and circumstances. They are all founded upon free choice. The Protestant, while he may miss much of great spiritual value, is not faced with an automatic penalty for not attending divine worship.

"A Catholic who through his own fault misses Mass on a Sunday or holy day of obligation commits a mortal sin" (*Baltimore Catechism*). The holy days of obligation in the United States are: Christmas, The Circumcision (January 1), Ascension Thursday (forty days after Easter), The Assumption (August 15), All Saints' Day (November 1), and The Immaculate Conception (December 8).

With regard to this and other precepts in relation to Roman Catholic Church members, the Protestant attitude is that these matters are strictly the internal business of the Roman Catholic Church.

ξ⋙

9. *Protestants believe that the financial support of the church and the clergy should represent a large part of one's Christian stewardship, and be on a purely voluntary (or pledge) basis; Roman Catholics stress the obligation of making financial contributions.*

Christian stewardship, the free gift of time, ability, talent, and money, is in the Protestant tradition of church support. Pledges are made, along with cash gifts, to provide for the current expenses and benevolent program of the church.

The Catholic, according to the law of the Church, "is obliged to bear his fair share of the financial burden of the Holy See, of the diocese, and of the parish."

Father McGuire, commenting on this requirement in *The New Baltimore Catechism and Mass*, says: "No Catholic can have true peace of conscience unless he is doing his share of paying for the expenses of his Church. Every Catholic, as a member of the Mystical Body of Christ, is strictly obliged, as far as his means allow him, to help the Church, at home and throughout the world, to preach the Gospel, to build and keep up the thousands of churches, schools, hospitals, and other religious works in which the Church is engaged."

"Mass stipends are given to the priest, not in payment for the spiritual benefits received, but as a means of his support" (*A Catechism of Christian Doctrine*, p. 240).

ॐ

10. *Protestants believe that "while there are indications of diversity in worship in the New Testament, nevertheless the preaching of the*

Word and the administration of Baptism and the Lord's Supper were everywhere marks of the Church's unity," and therefore nearly all Protestants have only two sacraments or ordinances, namely, Baptism and the Lord's Supper;[4] Roman Catholics have seven sacraments: Baptism, Confirmation, Holy Eucharist, Penance, Extreme Unction, Holy Orders, and Matrimony.

According to *Apologetics and Catholic Doctrine*, a textbook used in Roman Catholic schools and colleges, "The Church teaches solemnly: (1) that there are seven Sacraments . . . ; (2) that all the Sacraments were instituted by Christ Himself; (3) that they truly cause grace in him who is fit to receive them; (4) that the Sacraments of Baptism, Confirmation, and Holy Orders imprint a *character*, or indelible mark, on the soul, and that, therefore, they cannot be received more than once;

---

[4] A few "Protestants," such as the High Church Anglicans, think in terms of seven sacraments, although here the meaning of the term *sacrament* may not be identical with that held by Roman Catholics. There is, even within the area of the two sacraments held by Protestant churches, a wide divergence of interpretation.

(5) that, to confer a Sacrament validly, the minister must intend to do what the Church does, but it is not necessary that he be in the state of grace" (p. 126).

There are two kinds of grace; sanctifying grace and actual grace. The first, a sharing of the life of God, confers new life on souls. It is necessary for salvation; it is lost only through mortal sin. The second, actual grace, is "a supernatural help of God which enlightens our mind and strengthens our will to do good and to avoid evil." It is a divine impulse which moves a person to perform acts above his natural powers.

Christ gave the sacraments, according to the Roman Catholic Church, in order that men might receive grace through the instrument of divine power and love, and also that men might know, with certainty, just the moment when grace is received.

The Roman Catholic Church teaches that Christ himself instituted all seven of the sacraments, although some in a more general sense than others, "because He earned by His Passion, and marked off, the grace which each should confer, and because He personally appointed the several sacramental rites—in detail for Baptism and the Blessed

Eucharist, and in general outline for the rest" (*Apologetics and Catholic Doctrine*, p. 127).

Protestantism does not accept the seven sacraments defined by the Roman Catholic Church, because it finds only two, Baptism and the Lord's Supper, demanded by the teachings of Scripture.

While agreeing upon the number, Protestants do not agree upon the nature, form, or functions of the sacraments. Some reject the belief in the "real presence" in any physical form; others believe that Christ is present in the elements, that He is present when they are received, or that He is spiritually the Giver of them. Nearly all believe that Christ is present at the communion service in a real spiritual sense.

Some Protestants are now re-examining their own beliefs and practices concerning the Lord's Supper and Baptism. Do they, as now believed and practiced, truly manifest the will of Christ? In their present form, do they divide more than unite? Protestant leaders must find some formula which will give both fellowship and freedom of interpretation before the Lord's Table. As the Willingen missionary conference concluded: "Division in the church distorts its witness, frustrates its mission, and contradicts its own nature." It is therefore imperative that Protestantism join forces around the essentials which are held in common by its various denominations.

The word "sacrament" does not appear in the New Testament. Baptism and the Lord's Supper are essential beliefs of Protestants because they are specifically instituted by Christ. Their position is stated officially in the *Thirty-nine Articles* as follows: "There are two sacraments ordained by Christ. The five commonly called sacraments, that is, confirmation, penance, order, marriage, and extreme unction, are not to be counted for sacraments of the Gospel. They have no visible signs or ceremony ordained of God."

ॐ

11. *Protestants believe that baptism has certain saving spiritual qualities and is the door which leads to church membership; Roman Catholics believe that baptism is essential in order to obtain eternal salvation.*

Roman Catholics believe that Baptism is the sacrament that gives our souls the new life of sanctifying grace by which we become children of God and heirs of heaven. By means of sanctifying grace received in baptism we are spiritually reborn; we become members of the family of God, who becomes manifest as our Father in the supernatural order.

Baptism takes away original sin; and also actual sins and all the punishment due to them, if the person baptized is guilty of any actual sins and truly sorry for them. The effects of the character imprinted on the soul by Baptism are that those baptized become members of the Church, subject to its laws, and capable of receiving the other sacraments.

Baptism is necessary for the salvation of all men except martyrs. Those who through no fault of their own have not received the sacrament of Baptism can be saved through what is called baptism of blood (martyrdom) or baptism of desire (when one loves God above all things and desires to do all that is necessary for his salvation). Children should be baptized as soon as possible after birth. Infants who die without baptism do not suffer the punishments of those who die in mortal sin. They may enjoy a certain natural happiness, but they will not enjoy the supernatural joy of heaven.

The form of baptism differs among Protestants,

some accepting only adult baptism by immersion, others practicing infant baptism. Some Protestant churches practice both sprinkling and immersion.

"Baptism is not only a sign of profession, and mark of difference, whereby Christian men are discerned from others that be not christened, but it is also a sign of regeneration or newbirth, whereby, as by an instrument, they that receive Baptism rightly are grafted into the Church" (*Thirty-nine Articles*, No. 27).

According to the *Westminster Shorter Catechism*, "The sacraments become effectual means of salvation, not from any virtue in themselves or in him who does adminster them but only by the blessing of Christ and the working of his Spirit in them that by faith receive him." The *Westminster Confession* puts it this way: "It is a sin to condemn or neglect baptism, nevertheless grace and salvation are not so inseparably annexed unto it as that no person can be regenerated or saved without it."

ॐ

12. *Protestants believe that both elements of the Lord's Supper, that is, bread and wine, should be received by the communicant; the Roman*

Catholic Church reserves the wine exclusively to the clergy.

The Holy Eucharist is both a sacrament and a sacrifice. The Roman Catholic Church teaches that in the Holy Eucharist, under the appearance of bread and wine, the Lord Christ is contained, offered, and received. Christ instituted the Holy Eucharist at the Last Supper, the night before he died. When Our Lord said, "This is my body," the entire substance of the bread was changed into his body; and when he said, "This is my blood," the entire substance of the wine was changed into his blood.

In the Roman Catholic Church the priest in the Mass partakes of both elements, while the congregation partakes of the Eucharist under the appearance of bread alone. The Church believes it is unnecessary to serve both kinds, since Christ is complete in either element. After the priest has consumed "the Body and Blood of our Lord," those who are to receive Communion approach the altar rail. The priest then removes from the tabernacle the *ciborium*, which contains the "Sacred Hosts," and after absolving the people of their sins he administers the sacrament to those at the altar, saying,

"May the Body of our Lord Christ preserve your soul to everlasting life. Amen."

Protestant communicants receive both elements. After giving the members of the church at Corinth a warning not to abuse the Lord's Supper, Paul adds to the words of institution this comment: "For as often as ye eat this bread, and drink this cup, ye do show the Lord's death till he come. Wherefore, whosoever shall eat this bread, and drink this cup of the Lord, unworthily, shall be guilty of the body and blood of the Lord. But let a man examine himself, and so let him eat of that bread, and drink of that cup" (I Cor. 11:26-28).

While Protestants differ widely as to the interpretation of Christ's presence at the Lord's Table—from a memorial service to a sacramental ritual—they all believe that the true worshiper really meets Him there.

ॐ

13. *Protestants of various denominations believe that Christ is present at the Lord's Table in spirit, in or in conjunction with the elements; Roman Catholics believe that the bread and wine are actually changed by the miracle of*

transubstantiation into the material flesh and blood of Christ.

According to the Roman Catholic Church, after the substance of the bread and wine had been changed into our Lord's body and blood at the Last Supper, there remained only the appearances of bread and wine—that is, their color, taste, weight, shape, and whatever else appears to the senses. The change of the entire substance of the bread and wine into the body and blood of Christ is called transubstantiation. Jesus Christ is whole and entire both under the appearance of bread and under the appearance of wine. This change of bread and wine into the body and blood of Christ continues to be made in the Church by Jesus Christ, through the ministry of his priests.

For the Protestant viewpoint concerning the theory of transubstantiation, the *Thirty-nine Articles* have this to say: "Worthy receivers do inwardly by faith, really and truly, yet not carnally and corporally but spiritually, receive and feed upon Christ crucified and all the benefits of his death." Transubstantiation, as a miracle, is repudiated by Protestants.

In the Scriptures no mention is made of the

changing of the bread and wine into Christ's actual flesh and blood. Protestants believe that Christ was not here performing a physical miracle, but establishing a spiritual fellowship around the Lord's Table. Some Protestant churches, particularly the Lutherans, while rejecting the doctrine of transubstantiation, do believe that Christ appears in the elements of the Lord's Supper, with the elements of bread and wine retained. This is referred to as *consubstantiation.* In addition to the interpretation of the Lutherans, most Protestants believe that Christ is at the Lord's Supper in a spiritual sense. Here again we have to except High Church Episcopalians, who believe in the real presence in the same terms as the Roman Catholics, even accepting all that is implied in the word *transubstantiation.*

ॐ

14. *Protestants believe in the priesthood of all believers and believe that the clergy, although specially called and commissioned to special Christian service, is not of a nature different from that of the Christian laity; Roman Catholics make a sharp distinction between clergy and laity.*

The Council of Trent (1545-63) teaches that there is in the Roman Catholic Church a divinely instituted hierarchy consisting of bishops, priests, and deacons, and that bishops, having the power of confirming and ordaining, are superior to priests.

Roman Catholics call their priests "Father" because they are the usual ministers of baptism which, according to Catholic doctrine, gives them the new birth by supernatural grace, and also in his care for them the priest is the spiritual father of the faithful.

In 1896, Pope Leo XIII rejected the validity of the Anglican priesthood. The Roman Catholic Church, therefore, denies that the Anglican Church, or any other Protestant Church, has a valid ecclesiastical system and a properly ordained ministry. No Anglican clergyman, nor any other Protestant minister who would enter the Roman Catholic Church and desire to function as a clergyman, can officiate in the Roman Catholic Church without first being ordained by a Catholic bishop. (See *Are Anglican Ministers Catholic Priests?* by Francis Woodlock, Paulist Press, p. 8.)

Protestants believe that Christ created a "priesthood of all believers." They do not believe in a divinely appointed priesthood entirely separated from the regular members of the church. They ordain men, and in some instances women, to the Christian ministry, but they do not believe, in most cases, that the clergy is thereby given any peculiar spiritual powers exclusively its own.

Protestants generally make no distinction between the clergy and the laity as far as the membership of the church is concerned. They are equal from the standpoint of administration and authority. In many churches ecclesiastical government is not in the hands of the clergy, but in those of the laity. Here the clergy is called by the laity to serve the church in a special way, but it is still subject to the total membership. However, most Protestant churches believe in a (spiritually, if not administratively) specially "called" and trained ministry. There is a distinct feeling that clergymen are men of God, set apart for extraordinary Christian service. They are expected not only to live upright lives but also to be pastors, priests, administrators, personal counselors, and sometimes prophets.

Protestantism has no single theory of the Christian ministry. In some communions the clergyman is considered merely as a regular member of the church who has been called of God to render ecclesiastical services; in other communions a valid clergy consists of those who have been properly ordained by a bishop in line of apostolic succession. Churches having an episcopally ordained clergy usually place greater stress upon priestly orders.

Protestants declare that every Christian is called by Christ to be a minister, a servant of Christ (Acts 2:18). "Like living stones be yourselves built into a spiritual house to be a holy priesthood, to offer spiritual sacrifice to God through Jesus Christ (I Pet. 2:5).

15. *Protestants believe that no one has the right or power to forgive sins save God alone; the Roman Catholic Church teaches that the priest can and does forgive sins.*

It is the teaching of the Roman Catholic Church that Christ instituted a priesthood and gave to it particular powers, such as the power to forgive sins.

Pope Pius XI in his encyclical letter *Ad Catholici Sacerdotii*, written to the priests of the Roman Catholic Church in December, 1935, gives this function of the priest: "If he [the Christian] falls, the priest raises him up again in the name of God, and reconciles him to God with the Sacrament of Penance."

There are some Protestants who would hold that the clergy or priests have the authority to forgive sins. This is especially true of High Church Anglicans. However, the majority of Protestants believe that since every Christian is in Christ, and Christ is as close as breathing, there is no difficulty in direct communication and there is therefore no need of an extra person or priest to bring Christ near.

16. *Protestants believe that clergymen have the right to marry; the Roman Catholic Church enforces clerical celibacy.*

Celibacy is not a divine law of the Roman Catholic Church. But it is an obligatory law of the Western Church, imposed very largely for practical reasons—however, not solely, the "imitation of Christ" also being set forth as a consideration. After long experience the Church has concluded that a celibate clergy can do more effective work for God's people than a married clergy. For example, an unmarried priest is freer and far more independent than a minister with a wife and family. Besides, the specified duties of a priest would leave him little time for a family.

Roman Catholics believe that God helps the priest to remain chaste. Although they think of marriage as having a sacramental character, they also feel that there is special merit in a virgin life by one who gives his life to God for full-time service.

Celibacy is a voluntary matter as far as Protestantism is concerned. Most churches like to have a married man, for obvious reasons, as a spiritual leader. But many successful pastors are unmarried. It is entirely a personal matter.

17. *Protestants believe that one's total beliefs represent a "vocation" in the highest sense of that term, and also that the laity should have a prominent and official part in the life of the Church; Roman Catholics stress the sanctity of the priesthood and one distinctive, separate character of priesthood as "vocation" in an exclusive sense, and place the actual manage-*

*ment and control of the Church in the hands
of the hierarchy.*

In the Roman Catholic Church there is a sharp separation between clergy and laity. But while it seems to many Protestants that the Catholic Church is the clergy in action and that the laity has little or nothing to do but to obey, this is far from the truth. Individual members of the Catholic Church not only "assist," that is, follow or participate in the Mass; they take a very active part in the Mass and in Catholic Action and in the Confraternity of Christian Doctrine. Besides all this, an increasing number of Catholic organizations keep the individual members well occupied. The development of the lay apostolate is most interesting from a Protestant point of view.

It must always be kept in mind, however, that no matter how far the Catholic Church plans to go in creating a militant laity—and the current evidence indicates that it is going a long way—back of it all is the guidance of the hierarchy. Everything essential in the Roman Catholic Church must pass the test of the clergy. Faith and morals are under the "infallible guidance" of the Church.

And the ultimate authority, passing from priest to bishop, is the Holy Father at Rome.

Although the clergy governs the Roman Catholic Church, increasingly the laity is being challenged to help bring peace, charity, justice, to nations and to individuals. It is the contention of the Roman Catholic Church that the zealous apostolate of laymen will aid the salvation of the world. The faithful are being organized, locally, nationally, and internationally, to be missionaries, in a very special sense, for the Faith.

Protestantism exalts its laymen. It would be hopelessly crippled if all the positions of real authority were taken away from the laity. Its great strength lies in the active participation of its lay forces—men, women, and young people. Laymen are given positions of heavy official responsibility; they not only serve as elders, trustees, and deacons, but also teach and preach, and in some churches may administer the sacraments. Young people take upon themselves important Christian projects at home and abroad. Protestant women have been noted, along with the men, for their missionary zeal and programs.

All Christians belong to the Body of Christ. The church is a fellowship of those who have dedicated themselves to Christ (I Cor. 1:2). Therefore Protestantism teaches that laymen are called to specific Christian service within their own vocations, whether they are farmers, business men, scientists, politicians. In every phase of occupation the Christian layman is called upon to inject the Christian principles of honesty, unselfishness, and love (Eph. 5 and 6), thus making his daily life itself a Christian vocation.

ᔓᔒ

18. *Protestants believe, for the most part, that all people after death enter the state of either heaven or hell; Roman Catholics also believe in heaven and hell, but add an intermediary stage to heaven known as purgatory.*

Along with most other Christians, Roman Catholics believe in a literal heaven and hell. They also believe that there is a place called purgatory, and that indulgences are directly related to the time a person has to remain in the torments of purgatory.

It is the teaching of the Roman Catholic Church that death is a punishment for original sin; that the just who depart from this life free from all debt of temporal punishment are admitted at once to heaven. Heaven is a place and state of eternal happiness, the chief factor of which is the ability to see God face to face, an experience known as the Beatific Vision. Hell is also a place and a state —the place and state of eternal punishment which consists of (1) the separation from God (pain of loss) and (2) real punishment for sins (pain of sense). The torment is a physical reality, although it may not be caused by an element exactly like earthly fire. In hell the punishment is not equal for all, but corresponds to the sinner's deviation from God. Only those are punished in hell who depart this life with personal, grave, deliberate, and unrepented sin.

According to *A Catechism of Christian Doctrine*, "Those are punished for a time in purgatory who die in the state of grace but are guilty of venial sin, or have not fully satisfied for the temporal punishment due to their sins. There will be no purgatory after the general judgment. Since we do not know how long individual souls are detained in purgatory, there is need for persevering prayer for the repose of the souls of all who die after reaching the use of reason, except those who are canonized or beatified by the Church. The souls in purgatory are certain of entering heaven as soon as God's justice has been fully satisfied" (p. 143).

The Protestant and Roman Catholic conceptions of heaven and hell agree in general. Good works play a large part in the Roman Catholic system, while most Protestants believe in justification by faith as the way to heaven. Purgatory and indulgences are alien to the Protestant conception of salvation as constructed from New Testament teachings.

Jesus declared in Matthew 25:46 that "these shall go away into eternal punishment but the righteous into everlasting life." Protestants, basing their faith on this and other Scripture, think of eternal life as two separate states—heaven for the righteous, and hell for sinners (John 5:24)—although there are many interpretations of what these states mean.

Many Protestants believe that the doctrine of indulgences permits Catholics to "indulge in sin," and that this privilege of sinning without punishment can be bought with a price. This is not true. An indulgence, according to the official teaching of the Catholic Church, is not a pardon of sin; still less is it a permission to commit sin. It is rather a release from temporal punishment which is granted by the Church, outside of the Sacrament of Penance, to those whose sins have already been forgiven. While grace has been restored, usually there remain certain unpaid debts of temporal punishment. Some of these are cared for through penance following confession. The others must be paid for in purgatory by pain.

ॐ

19. *Protestants give a large measure of freedom, to both clergy and laity, in matters of doctrine and ecclesiastical practice; the Roman Catholic Church exercises the power of anathema and excommunication over all its members.*

Excommunication is an ecclesiastical censure, administered by bishops or the pope, which excludes a baptized person from communion of the faithful, with all the consequent disabilities and deprivations. Those fully excommunicated lose the right of attending divine service (although they still have to fulfill the obligations of the Roman Catholic Church; see p. 103, *A Catechism of Christian Doctrine*) and of receiving the sacraments, and have no share in indulgences, public prayer, and Mass (*A Catholic Dictionary*, p. 182).

Protestants, as well as Roman Catholics, have their creeds. And they also have their various tests and norms of correct belief. In order to belong to some Protestant churches a member must accept and not depart from the prescribed creedal position. Protestants, as well as Roman Catholics, have ways of punishing those who depart from orthodoxy. This, of course, is not true of all denominations. Some have no creeds, and only ask of their members acceptance of the New Testament as the basis of faith and life. Not a few churches give perfect freedom to their members to believe as they are led by facts and the spirit of truth.

Laymen, particularly, are making less and less of detailed creedal statements and are stressing the Christian way of life. Some feel free to join the church of their immediate locality, whether it coincides with the faith of their fathers or not. There is a tendency in many denominations to offer "open membership," placing all denominations upon an equal basis. This is not true of Roman Catholicism, which remains exclusive. Its creedal requirements remain unchanged. In this the Roman Catholic feels a sense of security and points to the conflicting creedal positions of Protestants as a measure of weakness.

20. *Protestants have no single ecclesiastical body which can adopt doctrines or church practices that are binding on all Protestant churches throughout the world; the Roman Catholic Church either through the pope, or councils called by him, can define dogmas which are absolutely binding upon every Roman Catholic throughout the world.*

The common idea of a dogma, meaning some arbitrary doctrine, imposed and generally believed, is not accepted by the Roman Catholic Church. It is rather a truth directly proposed by the Church as an article of divine revelation. It is truth revealed by God, according to Roman Catholic teaching, and therefore must be believed.

In defining a doctrine, making it binding upon all Catholics, the Roman Catholic Church does not create a new teaching. It merely makes clear something which has previously been a reality, although not fully understood.

Roman Catholics pride themselves on their freedom of belief. They point out that Catholics do not give a blind, degrading obedience to a fallible, human authority. They do not believe without reason. Instead, they find their freedom in gladly and willingly accepting a divine authority which offers only truth and protects against error.

Protestantism asks that each individual believe the fundamentals of Christianity. Belief, theology, deep convictions, are essential. But Protestants need not agree in every detail with all of their fellow members, and may even believe that church organization preceded the formation of the New Testament. Allowance is made for individual differences. Here, Protestants believe, lies their power. In diversity of views, within a central core of faith, they believe there is tremendous strength. In freedom of thought there is a creative foundation for intellectual and spiritual progress.

Fundamental to the Protestant position is freedom of conscience, with creedal statements serving more as directives than as hard and fast dogmas. Moreover, most Protestants accept the principle of progressive revelation, believing that while the Scriptures do contain fully the basis for Christian life and doctrine, there are new spiritual insights which break into history through the inspiration of the Spirit of Truth, individually, in each Christian.

Except in the great central convictions of faith, there is no uniformity of belief among Protestants. This right to believe and interpret Scripture as led by the Spirit of Truth is a fundamental New Testament principle. At the first council of the Christian Church held at Jerusalem, there was a serious difference of opinion (Acts 11 and 15). Paul did not always agree with Peter (Gal. 2:11). There were different views of missions in the early church (Acts 15:36-40). And while Christ called for unity of spirit, he never demanded uniformity of thought.

ॐ

21. *With a few exceptions, Protestants believe that most of the Bible precedes, and therefore determines the nature of the organized Church; Roman Catholics believe that the Church is prior to the Bible.*

Roman Catholics, while holding an exalted belief in the Scriptures as the Word of God, nevertheless place their Church itself ahead of the Old and New Testaments, from the standpoint of valid historical establishment. This is done on the grounds that it was the Church which after its own establishment determined which books of the Old and New Testaments were inspired and canonical, i.e., would comprise holy scripture, and that it is the Church which gives the only correct interpretation of the sacred pages. They believe that the Church not only existed before the New Testament, but was the mother of it.

After pointing out that Christ wrote nothing, and did not command that his apostles write anything, Father John A. O'Brien, in *The Faith of Millions*, goes on to say that the Church "is not the child of the Bible, as many non-Catholics imagine, but its mother. She derives neither her existence nor her teaching authority from the New Testament. She had both before the New Testament was born: she secured her being, her teachings, her authority *directly* from Jesus Christ" (p. 146).

Protestants and Roman Catholics agree that the Bible is the Word of God, that it is inspired, and that it is the basis for the Christian way of life. Tradition is accepted by some, yet not on the basis of divine authority. Protestants depart from Roman Catholic belief in the acceptance of the Church as the infallible interpreter of the Bible. They reject this position both on historical grounds and on the basis of personal experience. Most of them believe that the New Testament preceded and paved the way for what we know today as the Church. If it had not been for the letters of Paul, the Gospels, and the Book of Revelation, there might have been no Church at all, since a variety of churches were held together by the inspiration and admonitions of the various letters and messages.

Protestants believe that the Bible should come first because it is truly the Word of God. No man or institution, no matter how great, can supersede the Word. For Protestants it is the Living Word.

ॐ

22. *Protestants believe that the Scriptures are all-sufficient for Christian life and practice;[5] the Roman Catholic Church teaches that Tradition must be accepted along with the Scriptures as interpreted by the Church.*

The Roman Catholic Church teaches that the Bible is not the sole guide of faith. It adds the di-

---

[5] There are, however, Protestant groups and scholars eminently concerned with church tradition. Anglican scholars, in particular, have engaged in thorough study of patristic tradition, and have produced extensive translated and original literature in this area.

vine tradition committed to the Church. And it puts them not merely on an equal basis, but passes both through the divine authority of the Church. According to the *Baltimore Catechism*, "Tradition is the unwritten word of God—that body of truths revealed by God to the apostles, and not committed by them to writing but handed down by word of mouth. These truths, which were later committed to writing, particularly by the Fathers of the Church, have been preserved and handed down to the present day."

Roman Catholics do not find the chief means of salvation in reading the Bible as such, but rather in the sacraments of the Church. But the sacraments are based upon the scripture and tradition.

Protestants believe that the Bible is all-sufficient as a rule of faith and life. They accept it as God's Word and encourage its reading. Today, the Bible is the "best seller" of all books, religious or secular. To Protestants it contains inspiration and guidance, the revelation of the Son of God, the way to eternal salvation. John Wyclif stated the Protestant view when he said, "The sacred Scriptures contain all truth, all philosophy, all logic, all ethical teaching." The *Westminster Confession* declares that "the whole counsel of God, covering all things necessary for His own glory, man's salvation, faith and life, is either expressly set down in Scripture or by good and necessary consequence may be deduced from Scripture, unto which nothing at any time is to be added, whether by new revelations of the Spirit or traditions of men."

Wyclif put it this way: "Believers should ascertain for themselves what are the true matters of their faith by having the Scriptures in a language which all may understand, for the laws made by prelates are not to be received as matters of faith unless founded on the Scriptures."

23. *Protestants have a Bible of 66 books; Roman Catholics have a Bible of 72 books.*

The original writings of the inspired authors of the Bible have been lost, and the Scriptures have come down in the form of translations or versions. The important ancient Latin Vulgate version was almost entirely the work of St. Jerome, lasting from 383 to about 406 A.D., and undertaken at the command of Pope Damasus. The Council of Trent ordered the Vulgate to be held as "authentic in public readings, disputations, preachings and expositions." Roman Catholics believe that it conforms substantially with the originals and therefore contains no errors in faith and morals.

From the Roman Catholic point of view the term "canon" is applied to the list of books of the Bible officially recognized by the Catholic Church as inspired and containing the rule of faith and morals revealed by God. The Council of Trent placed seventy-two books of the Old and New Testaments in the canon. In addition to the books found in Protestant Bibles there were included Tobias, Judith, Wisdom, Ecclesiasticus, Baruch, and the two books of the Maccabees, with additions to the books of Esther and Daniel. These are known as the "deutero-canonical books."

Roman Catholics also have translations of the Bible in the vernacular. There are, in fact, several translations in English. Because of language changes, natural to all living tongues, from time to time more modern versions have been needed and have been produced. Catholic scholars, encouraged by Pope Pius XII (in the encyclical *Divino Afflante Spiritu*) to take recourse to the original languages and the application of recognized principles of textual criticism, are now working on an English version of the Old Testament; this will be followed by a direct translation of the New Testament.

ॐ

24. *Protestants believe that they have a right to read any version or translation of the Bible; the Roman Catholic Church forbids its members to read any version or translation not specifically authorized by itself.*

Roman Catholics are encouraged to practice what is within the Sacred Book, as well as to read it. After his ordination every priest is obliged to devote at least an hour every day to reading the Word of God. And Catholics believe that what is good for the clergy, in this respect, is also good for the laity.

Father Conway, in his *Question Box*, says, "They [Catholics] are not forbidden but encouraged to read the Bible. The Catholic Church, as the guardian and interpreter of the Scriptures, must needs prevent her people from being led astray by false translations of the Bible, which are often accompanied by glosses and notes destructive to the Catholic faith. But she never has prohibited versions in the vernacular which have been approved by the Bishops of the various countries, and have been edited with explanatory notes by Catholic scholars" (pp. 83-84).

In the front of the revision of the Challoner-Rheims version of the New Testament are found these words: "Pope Leo XIII granted to the faithful who shall read for at least a quarter of an hour the books of the Sacred Scripture with the veneration due to the Divine Word and as spiritual reading, an indulgence of 300 days" (*Preces et Pia Opera*, 645). Catholics do not have to read the Bible, for the Church takes care in various ways to give it to the faithful through liturgy and the sacraments. But in this granting of a 300-day indulgence, the Roman Catholic Church offers a practical inducement in order to make its members Bible readers.

On the basis of personal experience, Protestants know that the Word speaks to them from the pages of the Scriptures. There is no need of an official interpreter. As the New Testament books were written directly to the early Christians, in the vernacular, so should they be received today. The Bible is a great source of spiritual power for Protestants. It has convicted them of sin and sent them to their knees in prayer. It has brought them hope, comfort, courage, peace of soul, and salvation.

ॐ

25. *Protestants give the individual the right to interpret Scripture; the Roman Catholic Church insists upon being the interpreter for the individual.*

While every Roman Catholic is encouraged to read the Bible, no Catholic has the right of private, individual interpretation—unless it agrees with the teaching of the Roman Catholic Church, which serves as a supreme court. It is the interpretation of the Church which must be accepted. The Church alone, Catholics believe, can give the true, authentic interpretation.

According to James Cardinal Gibbons, in *The Faith of Our Fathers*, "The Church is the divinely appointed Custodian and Interpreter of the Bible. For, her office of infallible Guide were superfluous if each individual could interpret the Bible for himself. . . . God never intended the Bible to be the

Christian's rule of faith, independently of the living authority of the Church" (p. 63).

With the Church as an infallible interpreter of Scripture, every Catholic is absolutely sure that the interpretation is correct. This saves Catholics from the "errors" of many different interpretations, contradicting each other, such as are in evidence among the Protestant denominations.

Protestantism does not agree with the Roman Catholic conception of the Bible interpretation because it believes that each individual Christian has the God-given right to interpret the Holy Scriptures to the best of his ability, aided by tradition, the work of scholars, and the experience of pastors.

ॐ

26. *Protestants believe that Mary has a place of honor; Roman Catholics believe that Mary is to be venerated.*

About the only time in the course of the entire year when most Protestants hear about or take special notice of Mary is at Christmas time and Easter. Then it is in immediate reference to the birth of Christ, the Cross, and the resurrection of

Christ. But in the Roman Catholic Church great prominence is given to Mary every day of the year. She is exalted as the "Mother of God." Roman Catholics maintain that the *veneration* shown Mary is not the same as their *worship* of God.

According to the Roman Catholic Church, Mary is the mother of Christ. Christ is God. Therefore Mary is the mother of God. Her status is far above that of all the saints and angels. This is the reasoning of Roman Catholics concerning the Virgin Mary. It is supported all the way along by quotations from Scripture, tradition, and the church councils. It is the official teaching of the Roman Catholic Church that:

"The son of God was conceived and made man on Annunciation Day, the day on which the Angel Gabriel announced to the Blessed Virgin Mary that she was to be the Mother of God.

"The miraculous privileges accorded the Blessed Virgin Mary by Almighty God testify to her position as the most exalted of God's creatures.

"Because of her consent to accept the office of Mother of the Redeemer, and also because of her merits in intimately sharing the sufferings of her Divine Son for the salvation of mankind, the Blessed Virgin is given the title of Co-Redemptrix of the human race" (*A Catechism of Christian Doctrine,* p. 65).

Protestants exalt Mary and the Holy Family at the Christmas season. They worship with her during Holy Week at the foot of the Cross. They expect to meet her in heaven. Most of them think of Mary as the ideal mother and the human mother of Christ.

The Protestant point of view on the significance of Mary the mother of Jesus is based on scriptural grounds. See Matthew 1:18, also Luke 2:1-16; Luke 2:33, 44, 48; John 19:25-27; Acts 1:13-14. In none of these Scripture passages is there any indication of the Immaculate Conception, the Assumption, or Mary as "co-redemptrix." Mary is pictured as being rebuked by Jesus (John 2:4) and not sure of her own role (Luke 2:50). Protestants accept the New Testament version of Mary, which includes her beautiful song found in Luke 1:46-55.

Mary remains to Protestants the model of motherhood and they hold her in esteem every time they recite in the Apostles' Creed the words, "born of the Virgin Mary." Protestants, in creating their estimation of Mary, turn to the Scriptures where they find the following verses referring to her. In Luke 1:47 Mary claims God as her Saviour.

Elizabeth, in Luke 1:42, calls her "blessed among women." Christ, we learn in Luke 2:51, was subject to his parents. In John 2:4 and Matthew 12:46-50 we find that Jesus places Mary on the same level as any other mother, while placing his own mission above family ties.

27. *Protestants believe that Jesus had brothers and sisters; the Roman Catholic Church teaches that Mary had no other children besides Jesus.*

Protestants are of the opinion that Mary had other children in addition to Jesus, her first-born; but not so Roman Catholics. They believe that "Mary, the Mother of God, remained a virgin not only in the conception of Christ but also in his birth and during the rest of her life" (*Baltimore Catechism*).

Protestants read in Acts 1:14 that "these all continued with one accord in prayer and supplication with the women and Mary the mother of Jesus and his brothers." They will retain this basis of fellowship and association with the mother of

Jesus. Brothers and sisters of Jesus are mentioned in Matthew 13:55-56.

ॐ

28.   *Protestants generally teach in their creeds that Christ was born of the Virgin Mary; Roman Catholics believe not only in the Virgin Birth of Christ, but also in the immaculate conception of Mary.*

The Virgin Birth and the Immaculate Conception are considered, by the Roman Catholic Church, to be two separated doctrines. The first relates primarily to Christ and the Incarnation. The second refers entirely to Mary and relates to the condition of her *soul* at conception. It must also be understood that Catholics do not believe that Mary's own physical birth was supernatural—as in the case of the virgin birth of Jesus. She was born physically as any other person—only without the taint of original sin. The teaching of the Roman Catholic Church on this point is that "the Blessed Virgin Mary was preserved from original sin in view of the merits of her Divine Son; and this

privilege is called her Immaculate Conception"
(*Baltimore Catechism*).

The place of Mary in Protestantism is stated by
David Schaff in *Our Fathers' Faith and Ours*: "For
Protestants, the Roman figure of Mary is an ecclesiastical fiction which has grown with the centuries
until it was turned into a dogma by the arbitrary
utterance of Pius IX, that she was born without
sin. Mariology may have its historical significance
during the age of chivalry in exalting womanly
purity but the Scriptures have no syllable to justify
it" (p. 458).

࿔

29. *Protestants generally believe that Mary's body
was natural and must wait for the general
resurrection of the dead in Christ; the Roman
Catholics teach that Mary's physical body has
already ascended into heaven.*

Along with the Immaculate Conception of Mary,
is the dogma of the Assumption of Mary's physical
body to heaven. While this seems like a new dogma, being defined by Pope Pius XII in 1950, it
has existed and has been believed from the very
beginning.

Here again, Mary is unique among human beings. In the ordinary course of events death comes to every man as the result of original sin. Christ overcame sin and death on the Cross, and those who through baptism are born again have also, through Christ, conquered sin. Nevertheless, even the bodies of the just are corrupted and only at the Last Day are joined again with their redeemed souls. But this is not so with Mary. As Pope Pius XII explains it, "Now God has willed that the Blessed Virgin Mary should be exempted from this general rule. She, by an entirely unique privilege, completely overcame sin by her Immaculate Conception, and as a result she was not subject to the law of remaining in the corruption of the grave, and she did not have to wait until the end of time for the redemption of her body."

Having listed in detail many proofs of incorruption of Mary's body and its assumption into heaven, Pope Pius XII declares the following as a dogma of the Roman Catholic Church: "We pronounce, declare, and define it to be a divinely revealed dogma: that the Immaculate Mother of God, the ever Virgin Mary, having completed the course of her earthly life, was assumed body and soul into heavenly glory.

"Hence if anyone, which God forbid, should dare willfully to deny or to call into doubt that which We have defined, let him know that he has fallen completely from the divine and Catholic Faith."

Protestants are at a loss when it comes to appreciating the Roman Catholic attitude in regard to the Virgin Mary. They can understand how Roman Catholics might honor her and love her; but they cannot appreciate the so-called veneration of Mary, praying to her, requiring that all believe in her alleged immaculate conception, and her bodily assumption into heaven. Where in the Scriptures, they ask, can such dogmas find the slightest foundation of verification?

᠑ᢌ

30. *Protestants, with rare exceptions, do not direct prayers to Mary; Roman Catholics customarily direct their prayers to Mary as the "Mother of God."*

According to Roman Catholic teaching, the First Commandment does not forbid giving honor to Mary, provided that the honor given does not belong to God alone. Thus Mary can be venerated, but not worshiped.

"Our motive in commemorating Mary's name," says Cardinal Gibbons (*The Faith of Our Fathers*, p. 150) "is not merely to praise her, but still more to keep us in perpetual remembrance of our Lord's Incarnation, and to show our thankfulness to Him for the blessings wrought through that great mystery in which she was so prominent a figure. There is not a grain of incense offered to Mary which does not ascend to the throne of God Himself."

Thus the statues, the Angelus, the Rosary, the shrines, special processions, reference to her in the Eucharist, are all honors which bring the faithful nearer to God.

Do Roman Catholics pray to Mary? Catholics direct their prayers to Mary. They ask for help. And they seek her intercessory aid in carrying appeals to Christ himself. In this sense it can be said that Catholics pray to Mary, not as to God, but as to a powerful intermediator.

Catholics believe that Christ alone can redeem mankind. He alone can reconcile a person to God, making him a partaker of His grace now and in the hereafter. Moreover, they believe that no divine gift can reach an individual except through Christ and the merits of his sacrifice on the Cross.

Mary being no ordinary person or saint, and being so close to her Son, Jesus Christ, is in an especially good position to intercede for the faithful. Millions of Roman Catholics every day speak to Mary in the prayer of the Hail Mary:

"Hail Mary, full of grace! the Lord is with thee! blessed art thou amongst women; and blessed is the fruit of thy womb, Jesus. Holy Mary, Mother of God, pray for us sinners, now and at the hour of our death. Amen."

ॐ

31. *Protestants credit Mary with no miracles; Roman Catholics believe that Mary has performed and does perform miracles.*

Roman Catholics believe in miracles, and certainly in the miracles associated with Mary. Mary can perform miracles only as an instrument of God, not through her own power.

"No sooner had Pius IX proclaimed that we must believe by Catholic faith that Mary was free from the original stain, than the Virgin herself began those wonderful manifestations at Lourdes. It was then that those vast and magnificent temples to the Immaculate Mother of God were built, in which miracles are performed daily through the prayer of the Mother of God." These are the words of Pope Pius X in his encyclical letter *Ad Diem Illum* (1904).

Catholics believe that Mary not only gives them special blessings, performs miracles, and distributes heavenly gifts, but also, at certain times, reveals herself to the faithful. According to the *National Catholic Almanac*, some of her visits to earth occurred at the following places: Our Lady of Guadalupe, 1531, Mexico; Our Lady of the Miraculous Medal, 1830, France; Our Lady of La Salette, 1846, France; Our Lady of Lourdes, 1858, France; Our Lady of Fatima, 1917, Portugal; Our Lady of Beauraing, 1932-33, Belgium; and Our Lady of Banneux, 1933, Belgium.

ॐ

32. *Protestants believe that marriage is a holy institution and a sacred bond; Roman Catholics believe that the marriage of baptized persons constitutes a sacrament of the Church.*

Marriage, in the Roman Catholic Church, is a holy thing, and is raised to the position of a sacrament. The family gets its inspiration from Mary and the Holy Family.

Protestants and Roman Catholics agree very largely on the purpose and aims of marriage. They agree that the family is the basis of national life, and is of particular significance to the Christian Church. Roman Catholic marriage laws and regulations are spelled out by the Church in detail.

Thousands of men and women are being married every day. Outside of the Roman Catholic Church these marriages are on the basis of a civil contract, plus in many cases a religious ceremony. The Roman Catholic Church recognizes these couples as truly married; it even considers the marriage of *baptized* non-Catholics as a sacrament. And to Catholics the contract and the sacrament are inseparable—if the parties have been baptized.

According to *A Catechism of Christian Doctrine*, "Matrimony is the sacrament by which a baptized man and a baptized woman bind themselves for life in a lawful marriage and receive the grace to discharge their duties.

"Though unbaptized persons can be truly married, only baptized persons can be united in the sacrament of Matrimony and receive the graces of the sacrament. . . .

"We know from the constant tradition of the Church that marriage was made a sacrament by Our Lord sometime during His life on earth. . . .

"The sacrament of Matrimony is administered by the contracting parties, each of whom confers the sacrament on the other."

In answer to the question, "In whose presence do the laws of the Church require a Catholic to be married?" the *Baltimore Catechism* gives the following answer: "The laws of the Church require a Catholic to be married in the presence of the parish priest, or the bishop of the diocese, or a priest delegated by either of them, and before two witnesses. . . ."

Although Protestants do not consider marriage a sacrament, they do consider it a holy and sacred bond. They, too, seek to have a strong, solid family life. Protestants are in complete agreement with Roman Catholics that everything possible should be done to strengthen Christian family life and link it more closely to the Church. Therefore, they do not favor "mixed marriages" any more than do Roman Catholics.

౭๛

33. *Protestants warn against the dangers of mixed
    marriages, but have no specific church laws
    forbidding the marriage of Protestants to
    Roman Catholics; the Roman Catholic
    Church forbids mixed marriages and they are
    allowed only by special dispensation.*

Marriage to a non-Catholic is forbidden by the
Roman Catholic Church, and is tolerated only on
the basis of a specific dispensation. According to
the *Baltimore Catechism*, "The Church forbids
Catholics to marry non-Catholics because mixed
marriages often bring about family discord, loss of
faith on the part of the Catholic, and neglect of
the religious training of the children."

When, for grave reasons, the Roman Catholic
Church grants permission for a mixed marriage by
means of a dispensation, it demands that all danger
to the faith of the Catholic party be removed; that
the non-Catholic party must promise, in writing,
that he will not interfere with the faith of the
Catholic, and both must promise that all the children born of the marriage will be baptized in the

Roman Catholic Church alone and be educated solely in the Roman Catholic religion. On the other hand, the Catholic party must promise to strive for the conversion of the non-Catholic by prayer and good example.

34. *Protestants, under certain circumstances, permit divorces; the Roman Catholic Church teaches that a couple united in the sacrament of Matrimony can never, by any human power, be divorced.*

Under no circumstances will the Roman Catholic Church grant a divorce. In fact it does not recognize such a thing as divorce by any *human* power. This does not mean "that God cannot grant divorces for sufficient reasons" (Father Connel in *Matrimony*, p. 20). It is the teaching of the Church that "once a man and woman are completely united in the sacrament of Matrimony, they remain truly husband and wife until the death of either of them. A separation, a divorce, or an attempted marriage with another person does not destroy the marriage bond" (*Baltimore Catechism*).

While the Roman Catholic Church does not believe in divorce, it does believe in separation and annulment under certain conditions. It sometimes grants a separation of husband and wife because of cruelty or adultery, but will not permit either of them to marry again during the lifetime of the other. (In *Apologetics and Catholic Doctrine*, page 261, are named these other causes which justify a decree of separation: joining a non-Catholic sect; giving the children a non-Catholic education; living a criminal and ignominious life; causing grave danger to soul or body of the partner.)

After detailed examination the Holy See may reach the conclusion that a marriage which appears to be valid is, in reality, no true marriage. Such a decision is not a dissolution of the marriage bond; it is a declaration that as a matter of fact there never existed, even from the beginning, any real marriage. In the matter of annulment, the Church has the same laws for rich and poor alike.

Protestants turn to their Bibles to secure guidance for marriage, divorce, and family life. Jesus blessed the marriage at Cana with his presence (John 2:1-11). The home of Jesus serves as the model for the Christian family (Luke 2:51-52). And the home of Mary and Martha was a place of spiritual refreshment for the Master. The New Testament teaching on divorce (Matt. 5:31-32), where Christ permits a writ of divorce, in the case of adultery, is accepted by most Protestants as providing scriptural grounds for divorce.

While other "proof tests" may be pulled from the Bible to support Christian marriage and to discredit the practice of divorce, the chief strength of the Protestant position is to be found not in a few verses, but in the total impact of the teachings and spirit of the Scriptures. The development of Christian character and the practice of the teachings of love, forgiveness, and understanding are the best assurances of strong homes and happy marriages.

இ

35. *Protestants have no moral or spiritual laws forbidding the practice of birth control; the Roman Catholic Church forbids the use of any method of artificial birth control.*

The Roman Catholic Church considers birth control by artificial means as one of the principal enemies of marriage and the home. Roman Catholics are opposed to any form of birth control which violates the natural purpose of sexual intercourse, which is procreation. They do, however, permit couples to limit offspring by means of abstinence and continence. In other words, Catholic married couples are not required to have children to the utmost capacity of the mother for childbearing (Father Conway, *Question Box*, p. 339).

Nor are Roman Catholics forbidden to have sexual intercourse except for the sake of having children. This is its main purpose. But if it brings closer spiritual unity between husband and wife, even at times when conception is not likely to take place, it is allowed. The periodic (rhythm) method falls into this natural category. As Pope Pius XI has said (Encyclical letter on Christian Marriage, 1930), "Married people do not sin if they make use of their marital privileges in the proper manner, although at a time when, because of natural reasons either of time or of certain other defects, new life cannot be conceived, or is less likely to be conceived."

It is, however, considered unlawful and sinful for either husband or wife to prevent birth by use of any kind of chemical, mechanical, or other artificial means.

Pope Pius XI sums up the attitude of the Roman Catholic Church regarding birth control when he says (in the same encyclical), "Since, therefore, the conjugal act is destined primarily by nature for the begetting of children, those who in exercising it deliberately frustrate its natural power and purpose, sin against nature and commit a deed which is shameful and intrinsically vicious."

Birth control is usually not a theological issue in Protestant churches or homes. It is discussed on practical, as well as scientific and medical grounds. The World Council of Churches and many denominational groups have adopted official statements supporting planned parenthood in relation both to individuals and to the "population explosion" problem. On the whole, Protestant churches, while giving warnings and stressing limitations, take a favorable attitude toward the practice of "planned parenthood." Protestants can find in the Bible no moral law against birth control.

੩ঌ

36. *Protestants believe that Christ suffered "uniquely in His once-and-for-all death"; Roman Catholics believe that in the sacrifice*

*of the Mass "Christ through the ministry of
the priest, offers Himself to God in an unbloody manner under the appearance of bread
and wine."*

Protestants and Roman Catholics are probably
further apart in the celebration of the Mass than
at any other point. For here, as manifested in the
Protestant Reformation, there is a clash of conviction on essential principles. To the Roman Catholic the Mass is the very epitome of his faith; to the
Protestant it is something to be questioned.

"The Mass is the Sacrifice of the New Law in
which Christ, through the ministry of the priest,
offers Himself to God in an unbloody manner
under the appearance of bread and wine," is the
official definition as given in *A Catechism of Christian Doctrine* (p. 281).

The name "Mass" comes from the Latin word
Missa, meaning dismissal. In the early church it
was the signal, with the singing of. the *Ite Missa
Est*, that the entire sacrifice had been completed.
The sacrifice of the Mass is, according to Roman
Catholic teaching, the same sacrifice as the one on
the Cross because the Victim is the same, and the
principal Priest is the same, both being Jesus

Christ. Christ, though invisible, is the principal Minister, offering himself in the Mass. The actual priest is the visible, and secondary minister, who offers Christ in the Mass.

It is a grievous sin for a Roman Catholic to miss Mass on a Sunday or a Holy day of Obligation. This is the first commandment of the Roman Catholic Church.

After the priest in the Mass has consumed "the Body and Blood of our Lord," those who are to receive Communion approach the altar rail, where the congregation partakes of the Eucharist under the appearance of bread alone.

Protestants, with the exception of High Church Anglicans, do not accept Roman Catholic belief concerning the sacrifice of the Mass. They believe that the whole principle of the Mass is contrary to the teachings of the New Testament. They believe that Christ's death on the Cross, once and for all, is sufficient. Moreover, most Protestants do not accept the doctrine of the "real presence," that is, in bodily form. They believe that Christ comes to worshipers at Communion in various ways—along with the elements. Some believe in a physical presence. Most Protestants can see no advantage which might come through a miracle which does not already come to them by having Christ's real spirit present.

The Lord's Supper or Holy Communion, while being observed differently by various denominations, has a most significant place in the life of Protestant churches. Church members are richly blessed at the Communion Table in their spiritual fellowship with Christ. When all Protestants can agree to meet together at the Table, it will indicate that they have truly found their *living* Lord and are willing to share him spiritually with one another.

As far as Protestants can discover, the New Testament has nothing in it to justify the Mass as practiced by the Roman Catholic Church. While a few "high" Protestant churchmen use the term "Mass," the great majority of Protestants consider it contrary to the Scriptures.

ॐ

37. *Protestants practice a form of worship which, while corporate, is widely variable and individual, and they conduct their worship services in the vernacular; in the Roman Catholic*

Church worship is largely formalized and Latin is used almost exclusively.

Most Protestants, although understanding a number of features of the Roman Catholic faith with some measure of appreciation, are at a total loss when it comes to the Mass. For many Protestants the Mass seems, at first glance, almost sheer ritual, placed in a colorful setting and characterized by strange incantations in a foreign tongue. Catholics, however, understand it, appreciate it, and find spiritual life through it. The all-important functions of their Church are centered about it.

Latin is the universal language of the Roman Catholic Church. No matter where one may travel he will always find the same Latin and, nearly everywhere, the same form used in the Mass—although the trend is toward a wider use of the vernacular for certain portions. This makes the worshiper feel at home, and not a stranger. The Roman Church began at a time when Latin was the best-known language throughout the world. It is still used, not only for the practical purpose of communication with Rome, but to express the unity and harmony of all Catholics in matters of religion. For the benefit of the worshipers, so that they may better assist at the Mass, missals are printed in the vernacular.

ぷ

38. *Protestants are free to worship where they please; Roman Catholics are forbidden to worship in Protestant churches.*

According to the teaching of the Roman Catholic Church, "a Catholic sins against faith by infidelity, apostasy, heresy, indifferentism, and by taking part in non-Catholic worship" (*Baltimore Catechism*).

"A Catholic sins against faith by taking part in non-Catholic worship because he thus professes belief in a religion he knows is false" (*A Catechism of Christian Doctrine*, p. 171).

Protestants, on the other hand, are free to worship in any church.

ぷ

39. *Protestants, in the main, believe that God will receive to Himself unbaptized babies who die in infancy; the Roman Catholic Church*

*teaches that an infant dying unbaptized will
never be able to enter heaven.*

Roman Catholics make every effort, through the
sacraments of the Church particularly, to keep
souls from going to hell. They also go to the very
limit to keep babies from missing the eternal joys
of heaven, for it is the teaching of the Roman
Catholic Church that an unbaptized child is ex-
cluded from heaven. While it has not defined doctrines in regard to the specific fate of unbaptized
children, the general teaching of Roman Catholic
theologians is that they enjoy a state of natural
happiness in limbo where they know and love God
through their natural powers. Nevertheless, they
will never reach heaven and enjoy the Beatific
Vision.

In the *Manual for Nurses*, by Daniel E. Ostler,
O.F.S., published by the St. Anthony Guild Press
with the Imprimatur of the late Patri___ ___inal
Hayes of New York, this admo___
"The person who neglects___
danger of death is gu___
have to render an a___
of Jesus Christ___
soul is___

sin upon it. In such a state it can never see the Face of that God who created it, nor can it ever enter the Kingdom of Heaven for which it was destined" (p. 14).

Nurses are instructed to baptize the child when no priest can be reached in time. This will be a valid baptism so long as water is used along with the words, "I baptize thee—in the name of the Father and of the Son and of the Holy Ghost."

Most Protestants, on the contrary, believe that God will receive babies who die unbaptized; that they will enter heaven.

ॐ

40. *Protestants believe that full forgiveness of sins may be received from God and that it is not necessary for those who are forgiven to pay for sins after death; Roman Catholics believe that some sins cannot be entirely atoned rth and that the granting of indul- eviate the unpaid debts of t in purgatory.*

of the Roman Cath- for Catholics that

there is a purgatory. But additional proof is offered from the Books of Maccabees, from tradition, and arguments from reason. The reasoning is as follows: In the Bible it is stated that "there shall not enter into heaven anything defiled" (Rev. 21:27), and that "every idle word that men shall speak, they shall render an account of it in the day of judgment" (Matt. 12:36). On the basis of what we know about human nature, it is reasonable to say that many who die in grace are still burdened with venial sins. Such cannot possibly enter heaven and, since they are not enemies of God, they will not be sent to hell. Therefore there must exist a middle state in which the just can be purified and then proceed to heaven.

It is the teaching of the Roman Catholic Church that the time required in purgatory, to pay for venial sins, is shortened by the devotions of the faithful. "The faithful in earth, through the communion of saints, can relieve the sufferings of the souls in purgatory by prayer, fasting, and other good works, by indulgence, and by having Masses offered for them" (*A Catechism of Christian Doctrine*, p. 134).

There are two kinds of indulgences: *plenary*, which is the remission of all the temporal punishment due to sins; and *partial*, which is only remission of part of the punishment.

Heaven, for Protestants, is the final destination provided by Christ's atonement. All who accept Christ as their Saviour, and seek to follow him, will enter heaven. The test which Christ himself formulated is found in Matthew 25. Hell, for Protestants, is the place of eternal punishment for those who deny Christ in thought and deed.

According to David S. Schaff in *Our Fathers Faith and Ours*, "Protestant thinkers at the present day may feel some uncertainty in regard to the exact meaning of the Scriptures concerning the resurrection from the dead and the time when the future life begins but they agree in looking for the general judgment in accepting Christ's assurance that 'he that believeth on the Son has everlasting life,' and that no purgation in an intermediate realm awaits Christian believers after the present life" (p. 431).

Nowhere in the Bible do Protestants find any references to purgatory or to indulgences. Because they are not in the Bible, Protestants have from the beginning rejected such teaching. They believe that the way to heaven cannot be won on the basis of merits; it is achieved through the grace of Christ.

࿔

41. *Protestants believe that the Communion of Saints consists of "the fellowship of the whole company of believers on earth and in heaven"; Roman Catholics believe that it is "the union of the faithful on earth, the blessed in heaven, and the souls in purgatory."*

The official teaching of the Roman Catholic Church, as found in *A Catechism of Christian Doctrine*, is that: "By 'the communion of saints' is meant the union of the faithful on earth, the blessed in heaven, and the souls in purgatory, with Christ as their Head. The blessed in heaven comprise the Church triumphant; the souls in purgatory, the Church suffering; and the faithful on earth, the Church militant.

"Through the communion of saints, the blessed in heaven can help the souls in purgatory and the faithful on earth by praying for them. The prayers of the blessed in heaven are always efficacious because they are always in accord with God's will" (pp. 132-133).

For nearly all Protestants, the "communion of saints" means the fellowship of all believers on earth and in heaven.

"For we know that if our earthly house of this tabernacle were dissolved, we have a building of God, an house not made with hands, eternal in the heavens" (II Cor. 5:1). "And I saw a new heaven and a new earth: for the first heaven and the first earth were passed away" (Rev. 21:1).

ॐ

42. *Protestants believe that it is proper to confess sins to God and to each other, but that only God through Christ has the power to forgive sins; the Roman Catholic Church teaches that in the confessional the priest himself can absolve those who confess their sins.*

According to the teaching of the Roman Catholic Church, the sacrament of Baptism is absolutely essential. It frees the soul of original sin. However, there must also be forgiveness of sins committed after baptism. Another sacrament provides for this

purpose, the sacrament of Penance. Penance and the confessional go together, bringing to the Roman Catholic, in the confessional box, absolution.

Roman Catholics believe that the priest, properly ordained and authorized, has the power to forgive sins, and that this power comes directly from Christ. For Jesus said to his apostles, and to their successors, "Receive the Holy Spirit; whose sins you shall forgive, they are forgiven them; and whose sins you shall retain, they are retained." According to the Catholic Church, "no man, by his own power and authority, could possibly forgive sins. Only God can do that because sin is an offense against Him. But the priest, as God's representative, can forgive sins because God has given him the power to do so" (*A Catechism of Christian Doctrine*, p. 317).

Sins are forgiven when the priest says, "I absolve thee from thy sins in the name of the Father, and of the Son, and of the Holy Ghost. Amen."

The Catholic is required at times to go to confession and to confess his sins to the priest that he may find forgiveness. What sins must be confessed? The teaching of the Roman Catholic Church at this point is: "It is necessary to confess every mortal sin which has not been confessed and forgiven; it is not necessary to confess our venial sins, but it is better to do so" (*A Catechism of Christian Doctrine*, p. 317). The priest is bound—by natural, divine, and church law—to keep absolutely secret whatever he hears in confession.

From the Protestant point of view no one can forgive sins save Christ. God works through Christ to convert sinners. No extra intermediary is needed between God and man, except His Son. A relatively few Protestants provide for confession and permit the priest to pronounce absolution, e.g., some Anglicans, some Lutherans, and others. Protestants believe that God does forgive sins, and that Christ died on the Cross so that mankind might be saved. Confession, to the Protestant, is an outpouring of the heart to God, asking for forgiveness through Christ. This can happen at any time and at any place. God is good and he is more than ready to forgive those who seek him in humility and sincerity. Protestants are able to have contact with God and receive from him directly the forgiveness which a just and loving Heavenly Father feels they deserve.

Protestantism teaches that every believer has direct and immediate access to Christ, and to his throne of grace, and is assured of pardon quite apart from any priestly agency (Heb. 4:16). Forgiveness is a fundamental New Testament principle which asks that confession be made to God and to one another (Jas. 5:16). Jesus had a great deal to say about sin and the forgiveness of sins. In each case it was a matter of direct relationship with the Father (Matt. 23:4; Luke 11:46, 18:10-14; John 5:21; Mark 2:7; Rev. 1:18, 3:7).

〰

43. *Protestants tend to emphasize that prayer should be from the heart, directed to God himself, whether private or public, and thus they encourage personal, informal prayers; the Roman Catholic Church, while not ignoring informal prayer, provides an elaborate system of formal prayers to be recited.*

Much importance is placed upon personal devotion in the Roman Catholic Church. The Rosary, which is not only a series of prayers, but also a set of reflections and meditations, is one of the chief items in the personal devotional life of the Roman Catholic.

According to the Roman Catholic position, prayer is "the lifting up of our minds and hearts to God" (*Catechism*). Catholics, every time they pray, are asked to keep in mind these four intentions: to *adore* God; to *thank* him for his favors; to ask his *pardon* for sins and forgiveness of their punishments; to beg of him *graces* and *blessings* for one's self and for others.

In order to obtain God's help through prayer, the worshipers must pray with attention, with a conviction that they need God's help, with great desire for the graces they ask of God's goodness, and with perseverance. Distractions which are willful make prayers worthless. All prayers should begin and end with the sign of the cross, because the sign of the cross expresses two important mysteries: the Trinity and the Redemption.

Roman Catholics may use their own words in praying to God, and are encouraged to do so often. They are asked to learn the following by heart: The Lord's Prayer, the Hail Mary, the Apostles' Creed, the Confiteor, the Glory be to the Father, and the acts of faith, hope, charity, and contrition.

Roman Catholics have a wealth of devotional material coming down from saints and mystics through the centuries. These are made available in attractive, but inexpensive form at Catholic bookstores. Mass books, manuals of prayers, and other devotional helps are provided in very simple form so that they can be easily read, understood, and appreciated.

Roman Catholics permit personal, informal prayers. Protestants also have printed, formal prayers. While Roman Catholics attach particular indulgences to formal prayers and allow merits for this repetition, it must not be said that one type of prayer is "better" than another. In each case there must be the sincere attitude of the individual worshiper in addition to the words which are uttered. Formal worship and informal worship are therefore not to be paired off one against the other.

Protestants come very close to Roman Catholics in their devotional life. They both find Christ—through different channels. All Protestants are free to discover for themselves elements of devotion in various Christian forms. They need not worship at any special place or in any special manner. They may worship in a closet as well as at the altar. They may worship singularly, or in groups or congregations. Led by the Holy Spirit they seek God's presence in private and in their churches, and he speaks to them through prayer and through his Holy Word. In their seeking they find Him.

૨૦

44. *Protestants believe that true worship is devoid of physical objects having spiritual effectuality; Roman Catholics have "sacramentals" such as blessed beads, crucifixes, images, candles, holy water, medals, and scapulars.*

The sacramentals of the Roman Catholic Church are quite different from the sacraments, although they have, according to Catholics, certain sacramental qualities. But unlike the sacraments they cannot, of themselves, produce spiritual benefits. In *The New Baltimore Catechism and Mass*, No. 2, official Revised Edition, the chief kinds of sacramentals are listed as three: "(1) the *blessings* given by priests and bishops; (2) the *driving out* from persons or things *of the evil spirits* that possess them; (3) all *blessed objects*, such as: crucifixes, images, candles and so forth" (p. 202).

The Roman Catholic Church calls these "holy actions" and "things sacramental." They play an important part in the daily devotional life of the faithful. The prayers, the faith, and the devotion which accompany the sacramentals, and the pious thoughts which they inspire, are what bring the real blessings. The above Catechism points out very plainly that "to get any benefit from the sacramentals we must use them with true faith and piety; otherwise we shall be guilty of superstition."

Accepted on this basis the principal benefits obtained by the use of sacramentals are: actual grace; the forgiveness of venial sins; the remission of temporal punishment; health of body and material blessings; and protection from evil spirits. The most commonly used blessed objects of devotion are holy water, candles, ashes, palms, crucifixes; images of Christ, of the Virgin Mary, and of the saints; medals, rosaries, and scapulars.

Protestantism does not accept the sacramentals of the Roman Catholic Church, because they tend to make Christianity a mechanical affair and not something of the spirit. Protestants use physical aids to worship, such as pictures, stained glass windows, altars, communion tables, and various kinds of symbolism. But these do not have a "sacramental" nature as in the Roman Catholic Church.

Protestant worship is directed toward God and his Son Jesus Christ. Praise, prayer, the confession of sin, and meditation, communion, preaching, and the reading of Scripture, all find their proper place in the Protestant service of worship. In many of the churches, litany and beautiful sacred music add to the worship experience. At the center of most Protestant worship is the experience of the sermon. Congregational singing adds to the sense of participation. The Communion Table is present as a constant reminder of Christ's death on the Cross for the salvation of mankind.

Protestants stress a worship based upon spirit and truth, because this is the New Testament emphasis. Christ called for worship motivated by spirit and truth (John 4:23-24).

కు

45. *Protestants, with few exceptions, include Roman Catholics as members of the Christian fold; Roman Catholics slant much of their convert program in the direction of Protestants.*

Believing that it has the only true religion, the Roman Catholic Church has, from the beginning, had an extensive world mission program in order to propagate the faith. In some cases it has won whole nations over to its belief. At other times it has become a powerful minority factor, always with the goal of increasing its membership until it wins all possible.

It was not until 1908 that the United States was officially taken from the list of the Church's mission territories. But by that time the Roman Catholic Church here had already begun its own home and foreign mission work. Today it has an extensive missionary program, with several rather new developments including the Outdoor Apostolate, a mission project with the purpose of extending the influence of the Roman Catholic Church particularly in rural areas of the United States; Negro Missions; and Indian Missions.

Roman Catholic foreign missions are under the direction of the Congregation of Propaganda and of missionaries from among the secular clergy. Most of the older religious orders do missionary work. This is particularly true of the Dominicans and Franciscans. Jesuits are the largest missionary order.

Protestantism objects to the world mission program of the Roman Catholic Church not because it is unChristian, but because it is exclusively Roman Catholic. Protestants, like Roman Catholics, have a missionary program which reaches around the world. Both seek to bring the saving gospel of Christ to the "lost." Both seek "converts." They supplement their work of evangelism with that of social service and education, as do Catholics. In many respects this work of winning the world for Christ runs in parallel lines.

Protestants accept the principle of religious liberty for all, and in accordance with this basic principle they believe that a person has the right to change his religious faith, of his own free will and as his conscience directs, and that within every free state every religious organization must have the right to teach, preach, publish literature, and win converts. Protestants in America repudiate the claim that a single religious faith, either on the basis of dogma or inheritance, has the right to exclude other faiths from a free state, or that citizens of any nation are automatically born into a particular church.

ప

46. *Protestants freely permit their children to attend secular public schools; the Roman Cath-*

*olic Church forbids the attendance of Roman
Catholic children at "non-Catholic, neutral
or mixed schools," except by special ecclesiastical permission.*

Roman Catholics spend millions of dollars each
year in maintaining separate schools for their children. They do this as a matter of principle. They
believe that public schools, as they now exist in this
country, are not good enough for Catholic children.
Public schools are void of a true religious influence.

Back of the entire Roman Catholic school system, which consists of parochial or elementary
schools, secondary and normal schools, seminaries
and universities, is a basic philosophy of Christian
education. The official position of the Roman Catholic Church regarding education is found in the
Code of Canon Law, issued in 1918. In Section
XXII, these regulations are found:

"From childhood all the faithful must be so
educated that not only are they taught nothing
contrary to faith and morals, but that religious and
moral training takes the chief place" (*Canon
1372*).

"Catholic children must not attend non-Catholic, neutral or mixed schools. . . . It is for the bishop of the place alone to decide, according to the instructions of the Apostolic See, in what circumstances and with what precautions attendance at such schools may be tolerated without danger of perversion to the pupils" (*Canon 1374*).

Protestantism is emphatically opposed to the Roman Catholic teaching and practice regarding public and parochial schools because it believes in the public school system and holds that secular education can be religious in principle without church support or control.

While most Protestant denominations are firm supporters of the U.S. Supreme Court decisions in regard to the separation of sectarian religion from the public school system, there is a growing demand for more moral and ethical teaching in the public schools. Some even have their own sectarian day schools, feeling a need for more religious teaching.

ᔧ

47. *Protestants take the stand, on the basis of the separation of Church and State, that public tax money should not be used to support religious or parochial schools; Roman Catho-*

lics encourage the use of public funds for parochial schools on the principle that it is the duty of the State to help support the cause of true religion.

One of the sharpest points of conflict between Protestants and Roman Catholics in the United States comes in the area of public support for private schools. The issue of federal aid to education is one of the most critical elements in the conflict between Roman Catholics and Protestants, although there are individual Roman Catholics who believe that tax funds should not be used for private schools. On the other hand, there are a few Protestants who believe that private or parochial schools should have tax support.

Catholic authorities, backed by the basic principles of the Roman Catholic Church, maintain that laws—local, state, and national—which now prohibit the use of public funds for the support of "auxiliary services" for private or parochial schools are "unjust and discriminatory." This is because, from the Catholic position, these prohibitory laws arbitrarily deny tax aid to Catholic schools which, like public schools, prepare children for the responsibilities of American citizenship.

Roman Catholic leaders see no reason why the inclusion of religious instruction in a school system or curriculum should deprive it of tax support, just so long as it meets all the requirements of the compulsory educational laws. Catholics have objected to federal legislation which requires some states to use all federal funds for public schools exclusively. They maintain that a fair and equitable federal aid law must be based upon the principle that money appropriated for all children should benefit *all* children.

Many individual Roman Catholics advocate the use of public funds not merely for auxiliary aid, such as books, health benefits, use of buses, and lunches, but also for the actual support of the program and maintenance of both Protestant and Roman Catholic schools. Most Protestants are intensely opposed to this, since it violates, according to their way of thinking, the principle of Church and State relationship as found in the First Amendment of the Constitution. But, even more basically, they are convinced that the public schools are the chief agency for developing the democratic spirit which is found so uniquely in this country.

Protestants support the right of Roman Catholics to have their own schools. They reserve the same right to have their own private schools. But most of them do not believe that either Protestant or Roman Catholic schools should have, in full or in part, financial aid from the public treasury. Protestants support as a policy one system of public schools which are provided, out of tax funds, for all the children of the nation. This does not mean that Protestants want a purely secular school system with no trace of morality or religion. Protestants desire a public school system which is morally sound and which imparts knowledge regarding the general background of religion. They look to the Church School and weekday religious education to provide specific religious and sectarian instruction, and to win and develop personal loyalty.

Even if Protestant schools were included in some legislation for financial aid to parochial schools, it would be opposed because, they believe, by the very acceptance of tax funds they would be doing a disservice to democracy and violating an American principle. This is the principle which protects religious liberty and keeps our churches free. When they speak of separation, Protestants intend that neither Church nor State will be the master of the other.

48. *Protestants have no legal and binding arrangements with governments; the Roman Catholic Church has an arrangement of treaties or "concordats" with specific governments.*

The Roman Catholic Church is neutral as far as various forms of governments are concerned, except when they threaten the moral and spiritual life of the faithful, as in the case of Communism. In principle, it is above secular politics.

This is brought out most forcefully in the encyclical letter of Pope Leo XIII, "Christian Democracy" (*Graves de Communi*), in which he warns Christian action groups against becoming political parties. He asks all Roman Catholics to submit to the just commands of the rulers of the State. In another encyclical letter, "On Civil Government" (*Diuturnum*), he leaves the form of government with the choice of the people. But when there is a conflict between Church and State, in regard to the matter of unjust laws, the Catholic must obey God rather than Caesar.

A concordat is a treaty between the Holy See

and a sovereign nation concerning the interests of religion. Here the spiritual welfare of Roman Catholics is the first concern. The concordat does not necessarily mean that the Vatican approves the government or political system involved.

The Treaty of the Lateran, made between the Vatican and Italy in 1929, and incorporated into the constitution of the new Italian republic after World War II, made the Catholic faith the religion of Italy, and guaranteed its free exercise. The Italian constitution, although it recognizes Catholicism as the state religion, grants freedom to other faiths. While the Roman Catholic Church is primarily a faith and a religious institution, the pope is also sovereign ruler of a small area within the city of Rome known as the Vatican State.

Protestantism developed very largely in the environment of democracy. It is strongly opposed to the Roman Catholic position regarding Church and State because it firmly believes that there must be a free church in a free state, without preferential treatment of any kind whatsoever to any church, sect, or religion—and it feels that such freedom does not prevail for other churches and church members within most predominately Roman Catholic countries.

ॐ

49. *Protestants have no independent and sovereign government of their own; Roman Catholics have the Vatican City State of which the
pope is the absolute ruler and to which repre-
sentatives of other governments are accredited.*

The Lateran Treaty, in 1929, brought into being the independent and sovereign Vatican City
State. It is governed by the pope, who has full leg-
islative, executive, and judicial powers. It is also
perpetually neutral and extra-national and enjoys
all the rights and privileges of a sovereign nation,
including diplomatic immunity.

The State of Vatican City comprises 108.7 acres.
This territory includes principally the Vatican pal-
ace, its gardens and annexes, the basilica and
piazza of St. Peter and the contiguous buildings. It
has a population of less than a thousand, most of
whom are clerics. It has its own post office, news-
paper, radio station, etc. The pope delegates the
actual management of Vatican City to a governor,
who is a layman, and there is also a consultative
council, all named by the pope.

Pope Pius XI, when he took over the territory, declared, "It will, we hope, be clear that the Sovereign Pontiff has no more material territory than is indispensable for him if he is to exercise the spiritual power entrusted to him for the good of mankind . . . we are pleased that the material domain is reduced to so small an extent."

According to *A Catechism of Christian Doctrine*, "The present position of the Pope, as head of the Vatican City, shows to the world that he and his household are not subjects of other temporal powers. . . . The Pope's temporal power is a means to an end, guaranteeing that freedom of word and action which he must rightfully enjoy as the supreme spiritual ruler of the Church" (p. 125).

The late Cardinal Gibbons, in *A Retrospect of Fifty Years*, maintains that Catholics are not bound to obey the Pope if he should ever command them to be disloyal to their lawfully constituted civil authorities. "The Pope will take no such action . . . even though it is part of the Catholic Faith that he is infallible in the exercise of his teaching authority; but were he to do so, he would stand self-condemned, a transgressor of the law he himself promulgates" (p. 227).

Most Protestants believe that sending an official

U. S. representative to the Vatican is a violation of the principle of religious freedom and separation of Church and State. Sending a special envoy to the Vatican is to single out a particular faith for official recognition. Protestants protest against this, as they do against the official recognition of any or all religious faiths by the State. This does not mean that Protestants oppose the Roman Catholic religion as such; but it does mean that, although looking with favor upon close relationships between governments and churches, they believe there must be a mark of separation between the two. Otherwise the State might try to dominate the Church, or in some cases, the Church might actually control the State. From the Protestant point of view, true liberty cannot exist, either for the State or the Church, under such conditions.

ॐ

50. *Protestants, with perhaps a few regrettable exceptions, believe in, and practice, religious freedom for all faiths and for those of no particular faith; the Roman Catholic Church allows "equality of civil rights for all de-*

nominations," but it only "tolerates" what it consider to be false religions.

What Protestants mean by freedom of worship and what Roman Catholics mean by it are two quite different things. Freedom of religion, from the Roman Catholic point of view, is full liberty for the "one true religion." All other religions are in error, at most to be tolerated. This means that although Protestants may be given freedom to worship, the ideal situation is to have the State support Roman Catholicism as the official authorized religion in a completely Roman Catholic country.

This position is made clear in *A Catholic Dictionary* when it declares that freedom of worship is "the inalienable right of all men to worship God according to the teaching of the Catholic Church. No state can justifiably prevent the exercise of this right; and indeed it has a duty to foster this true worship. . . . But to avoid greater evil or to achieve a higher good, public authority can tolerate false religions, so long as they do not teach open immorality" (pp. 201-202).

Religious freedom, to the Protestant, is freedom to preach, worship, and to evangelize openly. It is the right to practice one's faith without government or church interference, so long as such practice does not injure others or endanger the State.

"Congress shall make no law respecting an establishment of religion or prohibiting the free exercise thereof or abridging the freedom of speech and the press." This is from the Constitution of the United States of America. The Supreme Court in several decisions has ruled that this "has erected a wall between church and state." These rights were written into the Constitution because Protestants brought to this nation, and championed, the cause of religious freedom. This was particularly true of Roger Williams who established Rhode Island upon the foundation of religious and civil liberty. Here he put into practice the principle of separation of Church and State which became a part of the legislation supported by the Founding Fathers. William Penn maintained that neither a good Christian nor a good citizen can be made by force. He therefore advocated toleration as the unifying factor of the New World. Virginia, largely due to Baptist influence, a few days before the Declaration of Independence was signed, abolished the state church and declared that all men are equally entitled "to the free exercise of their religion according to the dictates of their conscience."

෫෨

51. *Protestants believe the conscience of the individual Christian, plus the guidance of the home and church, should be the guide in the reading of books and the viewing of plays, movies, and television; the Roman Catholic Church has a formal system of censorship for all its members.*

An illustration of the control which the Roman Catholic Church has over her members around the world is afforded in the official *Index of Forbidden Books.* These books banned by the Vatican are forbidden everywhere and in whatever language they may be translated. Roman Catholics who publish, sell, loan, or keep them, without special permission, are subject to excommunication.

For the protection of the faith and morals of Catholics the Holy See issues, from time to time, a list of books which the faithful are forbidden to read. Another prohibition, but on a national basis and different level, is the list of forbidden motion pictures issued by the Legion of Decency, of the Committee on Motion Pictures, a special Bishops' committee. The *Index*, however, does not contain all the books which Roman Catholics are forbidden to read, but only those which have been placed before the Holy See for official action. Special permission may be received, for reasons considered valid, to read books listed on the *Index*.

Closely connected with the *Index* is the *Imprimatur*. Canon law demands that some books, such as those dealing with Holy Scripture, devotional and prayer books, and writings on matters of faith and morals, must have ecclesiastical censorship prior to publication. After such books have been examined by the diocesan censor and approved for Catholic readers, the term *nihil obstat* ("there is nothing objectionable") is granted. In granting this permission to have the book published, the Ordinary does not approve the contents *per se*. It does, however, indicate that the writing has already passed ecclesiastical censorship and therefore may be read by the faithful "without detriment to faith or morals."

Books which are forbidden reading according to the *Index*, as prescribed by canon law, are: editions of the Bible by non-Catholics; books which defend heresy and schism, books which attack religion or good morals; books by non-Catholics on religion, unless they do not contain anything contrary to the Catholic faith; commentaries, notes, and translations of the Bible published without Catholic approval; books which deride any Catholic dogma; books which, when dealing with the Masonic or similar secret orders, contend that these are useful and not opposed to the Roman Catholic Church; books which deal with obscene or impure topics; etc. Catholics are forbidden to read such books whether they are on the *Index* or not.

Protestants believe that the conscience of the individual Christian, in consultation with the church and home and aided by divine guidance, should be the determining agent in these matters.

᠉᠍

52. *Protestants have a world fellowship through various world alliances and through the World Council of Churches, but they have no central system of government or control; the Roman Catholic Church is organized as a hierarchy, with the pope as its supreme authority.*

In order to understand the Vatican and its world power, it may be helpful to have a few definitions of terms associated with the Vatican. *Holy See* means specifically the episcopal territory (or throne) of Rome, but in general has come to mean the pope as supreme pontiff, together with those who are associated with him in government at the Church's headquarters. *Papacy* means the office of the pope, or the system of ecclesiastical government in which supreme authority is vested in the pope. *Vatican* means the official residence of the pope at Rome, but figuratively it signifies the papal power and influence. *Hierarchy* (ecclesiastical) means the organization of the ranks and orders of the Roman Catholic clergy in successive grades.

In the composition of the Catholic hierarchy, the pope is at the head of the governing body of the Roman Catholic Church. The College of Cardinals serves as the Senate of the pope. It assists him in the government of the Church, the cardinals being his chief advisers and helpers. An archbishop serves as the bishop of an archdiocese and has authority, which is limited and defined by canon law, over the bishops of the dioceses of a defined territory (province). Bishops are the supreme ecclesiastical rulers of their respective dioceses.

Consistories are assemblies of cardinals presided over by the pope. A Council is an assembly of the Catholic Church, called together by its lawful head, to decide questions concerning faith, morals, or ecclesiastical discipline.

Although the pope has full and absolute jurisdiction in the governmental affairs of the Church, it is practically impossible for him to administer personally the affairs of the universal Church. Therefore, popes have established various groups of churchmen who are given particular areas of responsibility.

Protestants may disapprove of the power and authority of the Roman Catholic Church, but they cannot justly condemn a church *as a church* no matter how powerful it becomes. Protestants may not like the system of the Roman hierarchy, but that is a matter for Roman Catholics to accept or reject, not Protestants. Protestants do have a concern when the Roman Catholic hierarchy begins to take over functions, responsibilities, revenue, and sometimes property, outside its own sphere. Most Protestants believe that public property and common tax funds should not be used for any church.

It is not possible to reconcile the power and hierarchy of the Roman Catholic Church and papal claim with the teaching of Scripture or the practice of the early church through the first seven ecumenical councils. While we find reference in the New Testament to various church officers and grades of authority, it is very difficult to make these references add up to the establishment of any kind of ecclesiastical hierarchy specifically culminating in papal authority. The first Christians met, not in a great cathedral, but in a private home. The New Testament teaches that domination, unbalanced authority, or preferred position, are not attributes of the Christian Church.

Without any implications that the World Council of Churches is a super-church, a hierarchy, or even has power over its constituent members, it is, so to speak, the Protestant alternative to the Vatican—and is, of course, utterly different, in organization, program, and spirit. The World Council of Churches is not an ecclesiastical institution in that it has any of the powers or attributes of a church. It is composed of denominational groups and serves them. It works toward closer Christian unity. It is exactly what its name indicates, a *council of churches*. The basis of membership is that any church body which "accepts Jesus Christ as God and Saviour" may become a member.

This program of practical Christian co-operation, as represented in the World Council of Churches, is significant: (1) relief action on behalf of the war-stricken churches; (2) upholding the Christian standard of conduct toward friend and foe; (3) organizing interchurch aid looking toward rehabilitation of church life; (4) co-ordinating services for refugees and displaced persons; (5) enlisting youth in the Christian world community; (6) building a world fellowship in Christ of men of good will; (7) giving Protestant Christendom a united voice and a center of united action. One of its important contributions has been a detailed study and clarification of theological doctrines, carried on by the Commission on Faith and Order.

ॐ

53. *Protestants believe in Christian co-operation and are making progress toward various forms of church unity, although denominational bodies retain autonomy; the Roman Catholic Church believes itself to be "the one true Church," and will consider union only on the basis of a return to its own fold.*

Protestants and Roman Catholics have many things in common. They both have Christ as Lord and Saviour; they are both of the Christian tradition; they both have at least two sacraments, Baptism and the Lord's Supper; they share many hymns together; and much of their devotional literature, including the Bible, is the spiritual heritage of both. These, and many works of mercy, such as working together for refugees and world relief, indicate that Protestants and Catholics are not so far apart as many would have us believe.

The Roman Catholic Church insists upon union, that is, union with it as the "one true church." Protestants, on the other hand, do not insist upon any such organic union, and can find a real sense of Christian unity even in spite of their differences. Most Protestants believe in some kind of unity on the basis of Christian fellowship, but not in a super-church.

The Roman Catholic Church has established certain basic principles which, from the Protestant standpoint, do not make for church unity. Whether all Christians can ever unite on the basis proposed so often by the various popes, that is, for Protestants to reunite with "the one true Church," is exceedingly doubtful—unless new definitions and new practices are worked out. However, on the basis of Christ's own test, these Christians, who have so much in common, should find ways and means, without compromising their fundamental convictions, of having fellowship together and working in common for the great principles of the Kingdom.

From the Protestant point of view, the reality of a united Christian force, i.e., unity of Christian groups in spirit, good will, and co-operative endeavor (as distinguished from ecclesiastical, organic church union), is something to be greatly desired and sought after. Great progress has been made in bringing together denominations of similar belief and practice, and also in interdenominational co-operation. It is true that during recent years popes have extended to Protestants invitations to reunite with "the one true Church." Pope John XXIII has done this in connection with his Vatican "ecumenical" council. What must be understood here is that such a union would have to take place purely on Roman Catholic terms. In other words, it would be a *return* and not a reunion. Under these circumstances the best plan for Protestantism is to strengthen and to unite as far as possible its own forces.

Whether the Roman Catholic-Protestant dialogue will lead to eventual agreement in areas now marked by theological and dogmatic disagreement, it is hardly possible yet to say. But that co-operation in charitable work, growth of mutual respect, and a certain unity of Christian effort are within our present reach, we know—for, "There is one body and one Spirit, even as ye are called in one hope of your calling; one Lord, one faith, one baptism, one God and Father of all, who is above all, and through all, and in you all" (Eph. 4:4-6).